TOP

Six Sessions to a Better Career

Kern Peng

2020

Pike Publications
Cupertino, California, USA

Copyright © 2020 by Kern Peng. All rights reserved.
Library of Congress Control Number: 2019957850

Published by Pike Publications, Cupertino, California.

Cover image and design: Elena Peng

No part of this publication may be reproduced, stored in a retrieval system, distributed, or transmitted in any form or by any means, including photocopying, recording, or other electronic or mechanical methods, without the prior written permission of the publisher, except in the case of brief quotations embodied in critical reviews and certain other noncommercial uses permitted by copyright law. For permission to photocopy or use material electronically from this book, please access www.copyright.com or contact the Copyright Clearance Center, Inc. 222 Rosewood Drive, Danvers, MA 01923, (978) 750-8400, fax (978) 646-8600.

While best efforts have been made in preparing this book, the author and publisher cannot assume responsibility for the validity of all materials and the consequences of their use. The strategies, tools and advice contained herein may not be suitable for every situation.

The author and publisher have attempted to trace the copyright holders of all material used in this book and apologize to copyright holders if permission to publish in this form has not been obtained. If any copyright material has not been acknowledged, please let us know so we may rectify in any future reprint.

Author's email for this book: kerngpeng@gmail.com

Publisher's Cataloging-in-Publication data
Name: Peng, Kern, author.
Title: TOP: Six Sessions to a Better Career / Kern Peng.
Description: First trade hardcover original edition. | Cupertino, CA: Pike Publications, 2019.
Identifiers: LCCN 2019957850 | ISBN 978173355739 (hardcover) | ISBN 978173355722 (epub)
Subjects: LCSH: Career development | Vocational guidance | Counseling. | BISAC: EDUCATION / Counseling / Career Development. | BUSINESS & ECONOMICS / Careers / General.
Classification: LCC HF5549.5.C35 P46 2020 (print) | LCC HF5549.5.C35 (ebook) | DDC 650.14--dc23
LC record available at https://lccn.loc.gov/2019957850

Printed in the United States of America

First Edition, 2020

This book is dedicated to my wife Patricia,
who is my best career advisor,

and to my daughters, Ilena and Elena,
who are my best companions for learning.

Acknowledgments

I am very grateful to all those who helped and supported me in completing this book. Special thanks to Alvina Nishimoto for providing valuable feedback and editing, and Ginny Gray for her suggestions from the perspective of human resources management.

Ilena, my proud daughter, helped with proofreading and offered suggestions. She was the Editor-in-Chief of her high school award-winning El Estoque magazine. She is now a senior at George Washington University majoring in Journalism and Mass Communication. She has held various editorial positions at GW newspaper Hatchet and held internship positions at Narratively, Los Altos Town Crier, International Leadership Foundation and Federal Communications Commission.

Elena, my other lovely daughter, designed the cover of this book and helped improve the illustrations. She loves art and drawing. She is a junior at Monta Vista High School. She is the design lead for Yearbook, the art and web director of La Pluma, her school's literary magazine, and the design lead of Res Novae, her school's science magazine.

While completing this book during the COVID-19 stay at home order, I realized that being healthy is more important than having a good career. I would like to thank those who are fighting the COVID-19 virus on the front line to ensure our safety and health so that we can live our lives and do what we do.

Contents

Preface

Session 1: Strategizing Your Career Direction — **Page 1**
Introduction — *Page 2*
Developing talent — *Page 5*
Seeking opportunity — *Page 8*
Finding passion — *Page 12*
Exercise — *Page 19*

Session 2: Planning Your Career — **Page 21**
Vision — *Page 22*
Long-term plan — *Page 27*
Mid-term plan — *Page 31*
Short-term plan — *Page 34*
Exercise — *Page 39*

Session 3: Managing Your Time — **Page 45**
Understand bad behaviors — *Page 49*
Understand Your time — *Page 55*
Make time — *Page 58*
Exercises — *Page 65*

Session 4: Managing Your Tasks — **Page 71**
Prioritizing tasks — *Page 73*
Performing beyond expectations — *Page 83*
Managing risks — *Page 91*
Exercise — *Page 103*

Session 5: Managing Your Environment — **Page 107**
Managing relations — *Page 111*
Managing communication — *Page 135*
Managing situation — *Page 145*
Exercises — *Page 156*

Session 6: Learning and Education — **Page 161**
Continuing education — *Page 164*
Learning how to learn — *Page 169*
Becoming an expert — *Page 183*
Exercise — *Page 199*

Index by Question — **Page 205**
Bibliography — **Page 210**

About the Author

Dr. Kern Peng holds doctorate degrees in engineering and business: PhD in Mechanical Engineering specializing in nanocomposite materials, Doctorate of Business Administration in Operations Management and in Management Information Systems. He also holds an MBA in Computer Information Systems and a BS in Industrial Engineering. He has published three books solely in addition to this book and many papers in respected journals and forums such as Engineering Management Journal of IEE, Manufacturing Engineer of IEE, Journal of Advanced Materials, SEMATECH Manufacturing Management Symposium, and Tsinghua Business Review.

Dr. Peng is currently working at Intel, managing the Santa Clara Validation Center at Intel's headquarter in the Silicon Valley. He has over 30 years of management experience in engineering and manufacturing. He has been accorded more than 100 career awards in the areas of engineering design, software development, excursion resolution, project management and execution, teamwork, leadership and outstanding teaching. In addition to regular duties, he serves as a career advisor, mentor for managers, and new employee orientation instructor at Intel.

Since 2000, in addition to working full time at Intel, Dr. Peng has been part-time teaching at least two courses every quarter/semester term at Bay Area universities such as Stanford University, Santa Clara University, University of San Francisco, and San Jose State University. He has also traveled to Asia regularly teaching for Hong Kong University. In addition, he has taught courses and lectures for Shanghai Jiao Tong University, Tsinghua University, Zhejiang University, National Taiwan University, and University of California, Berkeley.

Preface

I have volunteered as a career advisor at Intel for many years. Through the online Intel Career Advisor Network and Career Connections, employees from different parts of the world have reached me for career guidance. No matter where they are, the desire of owning a career is unanimous. To reach more employees, I designed a course called Career Ownership and have been teaching it regularly. In addition, because I regularly teach part-time at several universities, I also provided career development advice to many students who took the initiative to ask. It is extremely rewarding to see my advisees and students achieving great accomplishments in their careers.

Recently, I completed my third book, *Project Management for Continuous Innovation*, which presents strategic models and practical tools for companies to achieve continuous success. Many of these models and tools were developed from my experience in career advising. There are striking resemblances between a company's strategic planning and an individual's career development planning. While I was writing the book for corporations, I felt that I should write another book for individuals.

I would not dare to claim that I have achieved success in my career. I am still on the path learning how to get there. In fact, many of my students have achieved greater success than I do, and there are many people who are more qualified to write about this topic than I am. Nevertheless, being a first-generation immigrant and having gone through an extensive learning and career journey in the United States, I have gained certain noteworthy experiences, and sharing them might help some people. With this simple motive, I decided to write this book and hope it will be somewhat helpful to those in need.

This book is organized into six sessions, modeled on how the advising sessions are conducted when an individual approaches me. Session 1 provides an overview of career development and the general direction through the TOP model. Session 2 guides individuals to plan their careers by mapping the long-term, mid-term and short-term activities. Session 3 introduces time management tactics to help individuals make time for career advancement. These tactics are quite different from conventional time management practices, and most people find my system unique and useful. Session 4 offers tips for individuals to effectively develop, prioritize and execute tasks, aiming to exceed the expectations of management, clients and colleagues. Session 5 helps individuals gain intelligence and sensitivity in managing work environments, including managing professional relations and navigating difficult situations. Finally, Session 6 emphasizes the need for continuing education and suggests methods for effective learning. This session is based on the lessons I learned from 35 years of schooling, from grade school to multiple doctorate programs, plus teaching at universities for the past 20 years. These lessons may be particularly beneficial to current students from high school, undergraduate to doctorate.

This book presents key information by embedding presentation slides in textual explanations. Readers can quickly obtain high-level information from the slides and read the details as needed to further understand the materials. The slides also provide convenience for those who wish to teach the materials of this book in a classroom setting. Furthermore, each section is headed with a question to be answered by the materials. A list of all questions and their associated page numbers are listed at the end of this book. This feature offers readers another option to obtain targeted information by reading the question and then finding the answer directly and quickly. In order to make the text more personalized, "we" refers to the advisee and I and "you" refers to the advisee.

While practicing the models and tools offered by this book, be flexible and adaptive according to your situation, as the recommendations may not be suitable for every single situation. I welcome your comments and feedback, which can be sent to my personal email at kerngpeng@gmail.com.

TOP

Six Sessions to a Better Career

Kern Peng

Six Sessions to a Better Career

Welcome and congratulations on proactively taking an ownership of your career. We will take you through the following six sessions to help you build a better career.

Session 1: Strategizing Your Career Direction

Session 2: Planning Your Career

Session 3: Managing Your Time

Session 4: Managing Your Tasks

Session 5: Managing Your Environment

Session 6: Learning and Education

Session 1

Strategizing Your Career Direction

High-level strategy for career planning

Session 1: Strategizing Your Career Direction

Introduction

- Career: A person's professional path or course of progress through life
- Career Development: An ongoing process of gaining knowledge and improving skills that will help an individual to establish a career plan

Career development can be explained by the TOP model:

Developing Talent (T)

Seeking Opportunity (O)

Finding Passion (P)

Slide 4

What is career? What is career development? Why take ownership of career development?

An average person spends about 40 years working, which is about 80,000 hours. How would you spend these hours? Whether you have an ambitious career goal or just try to make a living, you want to enjoy these hours as much as possible.

There are many variables in life that impact your career. Some people are lucky enough to be given a dream job with little effort while others fail despite hard work and aggressive pursuit. Working hard does not guarantee success so many people take the passive role, just following fate and letting nature take its course. Conversely, some people aggressively seek any possible opportunity and do whatever is necessary to move up. They sacrifice their family lives for their jobs but at the end many often regret. It is best to live a life with full experience in both career and personal pursuit, which requires careful planning and diligent actions. Not paying attention to your career will most likely limit the chance of success. On the other hand, aggressively taking on any opportunity without thoughtful deliberation will most likely cost more time and effort that otherwise can be used for other personal enjoyments. Overall, if you actively manage your career, you will have a better control and a higher chance of success, especially in today's fast and competitive economy.

Career in a Fast and Competitive Economy

- Today's success does not guarantee future employment nor success

- You will always have some control over your career

- You must accept risks and plan for the future to advance your career

- Pursue career security instead of job security

- The more you know, the greater your employability

- A commitment to lifelong learning will help keep you employable

Slide 5

Many things will change in a person's career and these changes are coming at a faster pace with bigger impacts. Instead of reacting to the changes, the individual should proactively plan his or her career. Before planning a career, we need to understand the components of a successful career. Let's explain this through the TOP model.

What are the key components of a successful career? What is the TOP model in career development?

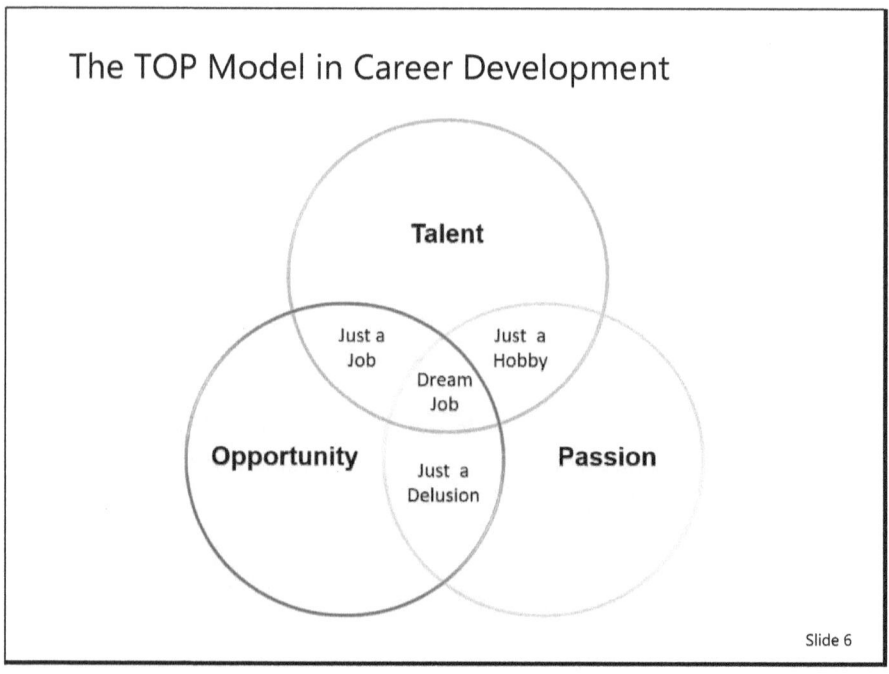

The TOP model was first suggested by Jim Collins, the author of *Good to Great* and *Built to Last* [1]. In the TOP model, shown on Slide #6, T stands for talent, O stands for opportunity, and P stands for passion. A person is most likely to be successful if he or she can land the dream job, which means the person has the passion for the job, the talent to do it well, and the job opportunity exists. When talent and opportunity overlap without passion, the person most likely can do the job well but it is just a job to bring money home for a living. When talent and passion overlap without the job opportunity, it is just a hobby that brings enjoyment but lacks financial support. When the opportunity and passion overlap without talent, it is just a delusion, since the individual does not have the skills to achieve successful results.

An individual should establish the passion circle first as it is where he or she has the most control. The next focus should be the talent circle which requires the most effort and the person has moderate control. An individual has the least control over the opportunity circle but can predict its change and movement by sharpen his or her acumen in the business environment and technology development.

> What are the characteristics of the talent circle? How should an individual manage his or her talent circle?

The Talent Circle

- Starts small when you are young and increases as you develop and learn
- Requires you to invest the most effort and hard work
- You have moderate control but not total control
- You may not be able to obtain certain talents regardless of how hard you try as they also depend on your natural strengths
- Develop strengths instead of weakness will optimize your success
- Continuous learning will increase your chance of career success

Slide 7

The talent circle is somewhat under the individual's control as he or she can choose their field of studies. However, since we are born with certain strengths and weaknesses, not all people can acquire the skill that they want. Some skills are just harder to obtain for certain individuals despite the amount of effort invested. This circle also increases over time as an individual develops and learns. A bigger talent circle results in a higher chance of being successful on the job and more importantly finding the dream job.

According the Marcus Buckingham and Donald Clifton in their book *Now, Discover Your Strengths*, it is a flawed assumption to believe that the greatest room for growth for a person is improving the individual's greatest weakness [2]. Buckingham and Clifton believe the opposite – an individual's greatest room for growth is in the areas of his or her greatest strengths. They also believe that a corporation should invest more efforts in the initial selection of their employees.

We can find evidence to support the notion of developing people's strengths versus weaknesses in sports. A TED talk by David Epstein pointed out that athletes get faster, better and stronger with world records constantly being broken. The winner of the 2012 Olympic marathon is nearly an hour and half faster than the winner of the 1904 Olympic marathon. Epstein stated that our human race did not evolve into a new species to warrant such improvements. One of the contributing factors is the selection of a specialized body type for a particular sport. He claimed that in the early half of the 20th century, coaches and physical education instructors selected athletes based on an ideal body build for all sports. Now there is an artificial selection for specialized bodies for different sports. In sports where a larger body type has advantages, the athletes got bigger, like American football. On the other hand, in sports like gymnastics where a more compact frame is ideal, the athletes got smaller [3]. Evidently, maximizing the natural strengths of certain body types has helped push forward overall athletic performance.

Just as an individual's physical strengths can be used to achieve greater performance in sports, an employee can utilize his or her cognitive strengths to achieve greater career performance as well. But what are the strengths for the success in the corporate world? Peter Drucker said, "Most Americans do not know what their strengths are. When you ask them, they look at you with a blank stare, or they respond in terms of subject knowledge, which is the wrong answer."

What are the natural strengths? How do you assess your strengths?

✓ **Assess Your Strengths**

- ☐ Achiever
- ☐ Activator
- ☐ Adaptability
- ☐ Analytical
- ☐ Arranger
- ☐ Belief
- ☐ Command
- ☐ Communication
- ☐ Competition
- ☐ Connectedness
- ☐ Context
- ☐ Deliberative
- ☐ Developer
- ☐ Discipline
- ☐ Empathy
- ☐ Fairness
- ☐ Focus
- ☐ Futuristic
- ☐ Harmony
- ☐ Ideation
- ☐ Inclusiveness
- ☐ Individualization
- ☐ Input
- ☐ Intellection
- ☐ Learner
- ☐ Maximizer
- ☐ Positivity
- ☐ Relator
- ☐ Responsibility
- ☐ Restorative
- ☐ Self-assurance
- ☐ Significance
- ☐ Strategic
- ☐ Woo (winning others over)

Source: *Now, Discover Your Strengths* by Marcus Buckingham and Donald Clifton [2]

Slide 8

In their book, Buckingham and Clifton offered three tools for people to build their lives around their strengths [2]. They called them revolutionary tools. The first is understanding how to distinguish natural talents from learned skills. The second is a system to identify prevailing talents. The third is a common language in describing the talents. Based on a study done by the Gallup Organization with over two million participants, they developed 34 themes of strengths shown on Slide #8. If you have not read Buckingham and Clifton's book, I highly recommend it. Taking the online StrengthsFinder assessment (https://www.gallupstrengthscenter.com/) may help you to discover your own strengths as well. People with certain personalities and strengths are more suitable for certain professions and positions.

After assessing your strengths, you need to assess your skills. Skills are gained by learning and are easier to acquire compared to strengths. We will discuss skill assessment in detail in Session 2 when we develop the career plan.

> What are the characteristics of the opportunity circle? How should an individual recognize the opportunity circle?

The Opportunity Circle

- Will shift, shrink or expand depending on the business environment and technology development
- The circle that an individual has the least control
- You may increase your career opportunity by building the business acumen of your chosen field
- You should not plan your career centered around the opportunity circle
- You may chase an opportunity but choosing a career based on passion is more effective over the long run
- The main tactic is to increase your awareness of the opportunities and make opportunities aware of you

Slide 9

The opportunity circle is also the most unpredictable one as it will shift, shrink or expand when business environment changes and technology develops. Chance is high that a job will change or may even be eliminated during the 40-year of employment of an individual. For instance, in the field of engineering, when I was in college, electronic engineering (EE) was very hot. Many of my friends went into the EE program but when they graduated, the hottest field was shifted to computer engineering (CE). Later, it was bioengineering, and recently it changed from data science to artificial intelligence (AI) currently. We will go through several of these changes in our career and we do not have much control over these changes. Should we just leave it to fate and do nothing? Of course not. We cannot stop the rain, but we can use an umbrella and forecasting when the rain comes is the key. Building the acumen of your chosen field will enable to see how the field evolves and which sub-area will be your next focus.

Many people chase the opportunity circle. They have the tendency to start their career planning by focusing on this circle. They select schools and pick majors that are in high demand so looking for a job will not be a problem. Often, it is a result of a family tradition starting at an early age as their parents typically push them to learn high-demand skills and even pick colleges and majors for them. Certainly, they gain the employability with the right skills which make up the talent circle, but what they get is just a job, a means to bring money home for a comfortable living. As a result, many lack the internal drive and self-motivation to push themselves to reach the top of their achievements. In other words, they do what they are told to do without internal drive and passion. Since their hearts are not into what they do, they do not push themselves to continuously learn and develop so eventually the opportunities are moving away from them. Also, it would be sad to spend about 40 years of employment on something that the individual does not love to do.

In the opposite, many parents let their children do whatever they enjoy and make them happy. As such, many pursue activities that align with their passion without considering the availability of job opportunities. A few people actually find their dream jobs because luckily some opportunities come along, while others end up with just hobbies. We should not count on luck and pursue a profession as a hobby. Unless you are independently wealthy, not having a good financial foundation, would not be as enjoyable as it should. While choosing a career based on passion builds the motivation for an individual to continue to invest in career advancement, each individual must be aware of potential opportunities to direct such effort intelligently.

Awareness in You and Awareness of You

- You need to be aware of where the opportunities are
    - Understand occupational outlook
    - Attend industry conferences
    - Join professional association and subscribe to their journals
    - Follow technology development
- Make yourself known in the circle so the opportunities are aware of you
    - Become an expert and be recognized as one
    - Network
    - Volunteer
    - Seek mentors and advisors

Slide 10

> What are the specific actions that an individual could take to increase his or her awareness?

The key to manage the opportunity circle is awareness. First, you need to aware where the opportunities are. For people in the early stage of their career, understanding of the occupational outlook helps them choose and plan their career. The Occupational Outlook Handbook (https://www.bls.gov/ooh/) published by the Bureau of Labor Statistics is an excellent source of information. For others, attending industry conferences, joining professional associations and reading their journals will gain the up-to-date information and the latest development in the field. In industries where the frequent technological changes significantly impact business performance, regularly reviewing emerging technology developments will gain insights of the new technologies and their trends. Reviewing the annual Hype Cycle [4] published by Gartner is a good starting point which sharpens one's acumen in latest emerging technologies. Keeping track of current technology developments will increase your ability to recognize potential disruptive technologies that can significantly change the career landscape of the field that you are in.

An individual must increase his or her visibility in his or her professional field and make himself or herself known in the circle. Essentially, you want to be the person who people are thinking of when they have opportunities available, which can be achieved in many ways. The first approach is through self-improvement by becoming an expert of the subject and being recognized as one in the field. However, not everyone can obtain such status as this requires extensive learning and practice. Although it is difficult, you should not give up as learning will help to increase your talent circle even if you do not gain the prestigious recognition. We will devote a session, Session 6, to discuss learning, not only for improving capability but also achieving an expert in a field.

The other approaches are through building relationships. You can make yourself known by networking, which means making personal connections to the experts and key decision makers in the field and at organizations that align with your career path. Another one is volunteering on projects and events in your chosen field. Volunteering provides opportunity to learn, especially when you are new in the field and a paid opportunity has yet been available to you. It also helps you to make connections to the people in the field. Finally, take an extra step into building deeper relationships by seeking mentors and regularly meeting with them to discuss and explore your career plan. We will discuss the details of establishing and managing professional relationships in Session 5.

> What are the characteristics of the passion circle? How should we define the passion circle?

Lastly, we discuss the passion circle, which is not required but at the same time a very important. It is not required because you can have a successful career when job opportunity is present, and you have the talent to do the job. In fact, many people manage to adopt and achieve comfortable livings with a career that they don't particularly like. However, if you want to live a great life, passion is extremely important. You only live once and spending about 80,000 hours on things that you don't love is a huge waste of your life.

> ## The Passion Circle
>
> - Not required but at the same time it is very important
> - You only live once so it is worthwhile to take action to identify your passion and pursue it
> - Only a few people find their passion at an early age, some never find theirs and many find it but do not actively pursue it
> - Passion is an endeavor that excites you to a degree that you are willing to devote a significant portion of your life to pursue
> - The most stable circle for an individual
> - The circle that an individual has the most control
>
> Slide 11

It would be great if you know your passion at a young age and just simply continue to follow your childhood dream when you grow up, but most people do not find their passion until they start their careers. Some people actually never find their passion. Many have found their passion but do not actively pursue it because they feel that either the investment is too high, or the timing is too late. Even if you are already in mid-career doing a job that you don't like, it is still worth to take actions to find your passion and pursue it.

It is never too late to pursue your passion as you may still be able to achieve greatness. There are many late bloomer success stories. Harry Bernstein started writing his famous book, *The Invisible Wall: A Love Story That Broke Barriers,* at the age of 93. Anna Robertson self-taught to become an American primitive artist in her seventies and became well-known as "Grandma Moses." Ray Kroc went into the restaurant business partnering with others at the age of 53, purchased the restaurant at the age of 59 and turned it into a successful empire known as McDonald's [5].

Now let's define passion. First, passion is what you enjoy doing but it may not be what you are good at doing, which is your strengths in the talent circle. Some people are born with certain abilities that make them suitable for performing certain activities but if they are not into those activities or losing interest quickly, they do not have the passion for those activities. Also, we may enjoy many things but not all of them become passions. Pablo Picasso said, "All children are artists, the problem is how to remain an artist once he grows up." Children show "passion" in many things, but it is not a real passion unless they stick to it after growing up. Therefore, passion is an endeavor that excites you to a degree that you are willing to devote a significant amount of effort and time to pursue. Among the three circles, the passion circle is the most stable one as an individual typically doesn't change passion often. It is rather personal and under the control of the individual. What to do with passion is all up to you. Many people have big dreams but if no action is taken, these are merely wishes and have nothing to do with passion. So, taking action is the key.

How to establish the passion circle?

The first action is to identify passion. The earlier you start the process, the more enjoyable you will find it, while being able to go further and reach higher success in your career. Ideally, you want to have your passion identified before you enter college so your talent circle will align with your passion. However, this is an iterative exploratory process and often you do not know for sure until you really experience it. I entered college with an Electronic Engineering (EE) major, and then changed to Mechanical Engineering (ME) but graduated with an Industrial Engineering (IE) degree, which was still not my final calling. It wasn't until working many years in the high-tech industry, I eventually found my passion in education. Searching for your passion takes time but as long as you don't give up, you will find it and when you do, it will be so rewarding that is well worth the effort.

Taking Actions to Find and Pursue Passion

- Taking actions to find your passion as early as possible, preferably when you are still in school

- Explore - Not all activities that you love will turn into passion. It takes time and effort to narrow down the ones you really love

- Start seeking passion from what you love but also from what you value and inspire to be

- Don't make excuses, make plan and take steps toward your career goals. Even if these action steps are small, they can eventually take you there

Slide 12

You should begin the passion searching process by identifying the activities that you enjoy doing. Of course, most of us enjoy doing many things and not all of them are related to your passion. There are many career assessment tests available online and the methodology behind these tests is using your likes and dislikes to identify a list of suitable jobs for you. When you take the test, you need to make the selection based on what excites you and not how well you can perform. It is a huge difference between what you love and what you can do skillfully.

Once you finish the test, you will have a preliminary list of potential professions but to find your true passion, you need to search your soul to understand what you value, and you aspire to be. To do this, you may list the people who you admire and write down what they did that truly inspire you. These people could be public heroes or relatives who you look up to.

Now you can review this list of people against the list of career test potential professions for similarities. For those people you personally know, having conversations with them will help you confirm what you really want to pursue. After identifying the possible pursuits, you should get some real experience. If possible, seek practice opportunities, or at a minimum, seek mentors and advisors who went through similar career paths. Once you further narrow down the choices, you then plan the specific action steps to achieve your goal.

As you execute your plan, you may find things change or you may change your goal as you discover the details. It is perfectly fine, and the entire process may take time and require iterative explorations. In the next session, we will discuss how to develop a career plan even if you are not sure what your passion is. At this moment, what we want is your commitment to take action. Don't make excuses, make a plan and take steps toward your career goals. Even if these steps are small, they can eventually take you where you want to be.

> ## Session 1 Summary: Applying the TOP Model
>
> - The TOP model is a strategic guide for career development, which is a process of attaining self-awareness, skills and opportunities to maximize the fulfillment of an individual's profession life
> - Establishing the passion circle should be the first step in career development
> - The talent circle is the next focus, which is a lifelong pursuit and takes the most effort to plan and execute
> - Survey the opportunity circle regularly and make adjustments accordingly to your plans and actions for the talent circle
>
> Slide 13

How to apply the TOP model in career development?

The TOP model provides a general guide for career development at the strategic level. It highlights that an individual should consider all three components to attain a fulfilling career.

Applying the TOP model, you need to first find your passion through a process of self-discovery. Next, you need to gain the talent that aligns with your passion and at the same time seek opportunities where the talent is applicable. This is the most effort-consuming process requiring you to identify your strengths and skills, and then develop short-term, mid-term and long-term plans so that your entire career roadmap is covered. More importantly, you must take actions to execute to these plans. Of course, these plans are subjected to change, rarely due to changes in passion and largely due to changes in the opportunity circle.

Therefore, you should regularly survey the opportunity circle, which means following the new developments of the industry and being aware of its future trend. Doing so, you can proactively make changes to the career plan and take actions to prepare for the future. You don't want to be in redeployment and find out that there is no job available for your skills.

The TOP model serves a simple purpose, guiding you to understand yourself as well as career market to plan accordingly. We will discuss how to plan your career in the next session.

Session 1 Exercise – Build your TOP model

Step 1. Self-understanding. Fill out the following boxes:

My passion: (Things that I enjoy doing)

1. _____

2. _____

3. _____

My talent: (Things that I am good at doing - strengths)

1. _____

2. _____

3. _____

4. _____

5. _____

My hobbies:

1. _____

2. _____

3. _____

Step 2. Opportunity finding. Think within your interested career areas and fill out the following boxes:

Current opportunities: (Available Jobs that I want to try)

1. _____

2. _____

3. _____

Future opportunities: (Jobs with increasing perspectives)

1. _____

2. _____

3. _____

4. _____

5. _____

Step 3. Finding your potential career goal. Do you see any of the above job opportunities that aligns with your hobbies?

My dream jobs:

1. _____

2. _____

3. _____

Session 2

Planning Your Career

Develop a career plan

> **Session 2: Planning Your Career**
>
> Before developing a plan, you must have a vision
>
> *Vision*
>
> - Career vision is an image of how your career should look like at its peak, the ideal career state you wish to be in
>
> Developing a career plan:
>
> - *Long-term plan*
> - *Mid-term plan*
> - *Short-term plan*
>
> Slide 15

> What is a career vision? Why is a career vision important?

A career vision is an aspirational picture of the future where you ultimately want to be. It is your dream job at its peak. We did an exercise in the last session identifying your potential career goal with a few dream jobs, which is a first step in finding your career vision. Your career vision may not stay the same and may change while you explore your options. As explained in the TOP model during last session, it will be impacted by your ability and the opportunities available to you and both are changing over time. Your career vison needs to be stretching and challenging while at the same time realistic and feasible.

A career vision serves three main purposes. The first is to provide a general direction for your career pursuit, like the North Star in the sky guiding you in the dark. The second is being a motivational instrument to help you see the light while walking through the difficult courses of your career journey. The last is a starting point for developing a step-by-step career plan with milestones to achieve great success that may seem overwhelmingly challenging at first.

Identifying and Developing a Career Vision

- Everyone is unique and the vision is personal
  - Individual who has a clear ideal state
    - move onto developing career plan
  - Individual with many ideal states
    - put the ideal states in time order
    - develop focused strategy
    - explore the possibility of multiple career paths
  - Individual does not have a clear vision
    - identify possible career progressions
    - develop a career vision aligned to passion
- An individual's career vision may change, and regular reviews and updates are needed

Slide 16

How does an individual identify and develop a career vision?

A career vision is unique to the individual. Everyone is unique and only the individual knows what he or she wants. When I take on a new advisee, I start by identifying his or her career vision. I generally ask, "what is your ideal position at the peak of your career?" Individuals answer this question differently. Some people know exactly what they want so it would be easier for us to move onto developing the career plan. However, most people do not have a straight answer. Some of them have many ideal cases and some do not have any. We will take different steps to help them develop their career visions.

People who describe many ideal states may have difficulty in deciding or may actually want everything. In this case, we need to help the individual develop a vision that is focused and not overwhelming at any given time. The approach is to put these ideal states in time perspective by asking the individual questions such as "which ideal state do you want to achieve first and by when?" or "could you put these ideal states into a preferred order for execution?" The intention is to help the individual realize that some ideal states can be combined, and others may be mapped into different periods on the career path so that the individual can set targets to achieve them one-by-one with the last one as the ultimate target. It would also be fine to have multiple ideal states with different career paths, like myself for example, I have been pursuing one in the corporate world and one in academia in parallel for decades. However, the individual must comprehend the full scope of work and take serious considerations when determining to pursue such a challenging mission. It is doable but requires substantial commitment and discipline in time and task management, which will be discuss in future sessions.

For individuals who do not have a clear vision of their career, we can guide them to see the possible progressions of their career. We could ask the individuals, "how do you see yourself in 5 years, 10 years, 15 years and 20 years from now?" While receiving their responses, we also need to help them connect their answers to their passions through a series of "why" questions. Passion is a key component for career success as discussed in the last session. Our intention is to help the individual to build the preliminary career vision that aligns with his or her passion. Another approach is asking the advisees about people who they admire. From their answers, we can see who they want to be and the position they want to hold. If the vision is still not clear, we can do the following exercise:

1) Ask the individual to list activities that he or she enjoys doing. Remind the individual that these activities are not necessarily what they are good at doing.
2) Based on the activities, identify career roles that actively engage in those activities.
3) Work with the individual to select one of the career roles as career vision.

An individual does not need to finalize a career vision to start developing a career plan. In fact, many people who are so certain of their career visions at times change their minds as their careers progress and opportunities develop. Just think about how many times we change our childhood dreams on what we want to be. Also, the career vision does not need to be realistic which is typically defined by current status quo. Do not set unnecessary limits to what can be achieved. The career vision is not set in stone and can change. However, the conversation on career vision is absolutely necessary as it provides a general direction for the career plan. As long as there is a preliminary vision, we can move onto developing a career plan, which may include exploratory activities to confirm or further define the clarity of that vision. This vision should be reviewed and updated regularly.

> What does a good career plan look like?

A good career plan should include actionable developmental activities mapped through time with long-term, mid-term and short-term subplans. Shown on Slide #17, the career planning chart has time on the x-axis and learning on the y-axis. An individual needs additional skills to reach the career vision and these skills can be progressively listed from the current competency to the advanced skills along the learning axis. By mapping the activities for obtaining these skills along the time axis, an overview of the individual's short-term, mid-term and long-term career plan is presented.

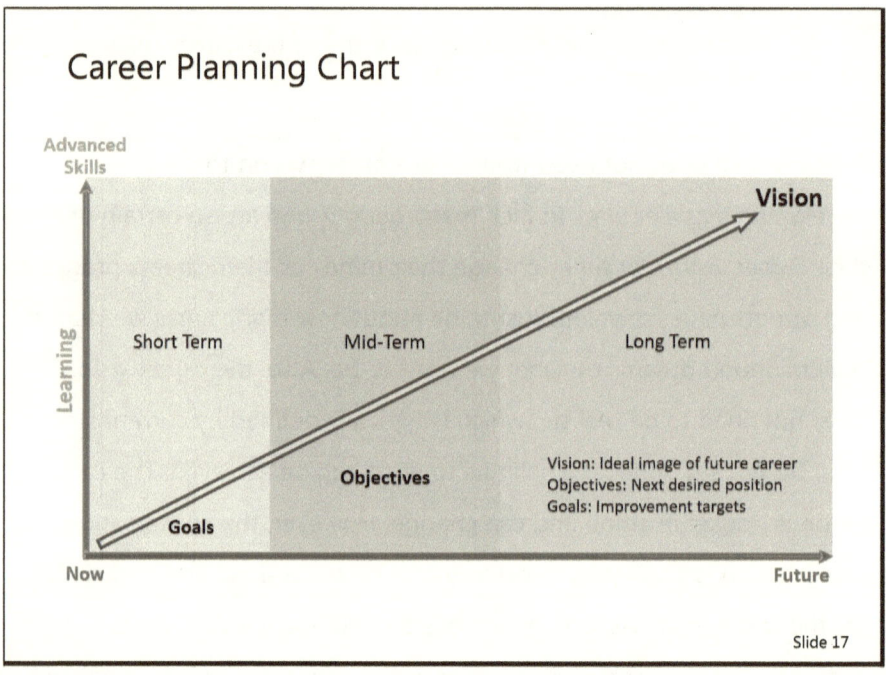

Drafting a career plan may start with copying the Career Planning Chart on a poster-size paper. We then typically write the learning activities on the chart or use Post-it notes to stick them on the poster based on the short-term, mid-term and long-term timeline. We will discuss the selection of the learning activities after we discuss the planning process. Once we are satisfied with the preliminary activities and their rough timeline, we then transfer them to an Excel format, like the one shown on Slide #18, for easier modification and better tracking of the progress. The short-term timeline is in months, the mid-term timeline is in quarters and the long-term timeline is in years. It looks like a Gantt chart in project management, but execution starts from the bottom row of the table and moves upward, aligning with the Career Planning Chart.

Career Planning Template Using Excel

Vision: Managing technical marketing of key product programs
Target Date: 2023

Knowledge Areas	Jan19	Feb19	Mar19	Apr19	May19	Jun19	Jul19	Aug19	Sep19	Oct19	Nov19	Dec19	Q1 20	Q2 20	Q3 20	Q4 20	2021	2022	2023
Strategic planning										Find a mentor			Meet with mentor quarterly						Develop strategic plan
HR & Management								HR connection					HR meeting				Class		Manager opportunity
Economics															Class				
Business laws															Book and class				
Client management															Book and class				
MBA degree						Explore				Back to school									
Finance/Accounting									Book or class										
Marketing			Mentor		Book			Book			Class		DOT		Class	Class			
Presentation skills		Toastmasters																	
Project management		Book		Class			PM opportunity			Manage projects			Adv. PM classes						
Time management	Book	Habit 1 change	Habit 2 change	Habit 3 change															
Time	Jan19	Feb19	Mar19	Apr19	May19	Jun19	Jul19	Aug19	Sep19	Oct19	Nov19	Dec19	Q1 20	Q2 20	Q3 20	Q4 20	2021	2022	2023

Goals:
1. Master time management within 1 month and map out habits to change.
2. Learn project management basics within 6 month and seek PM opportunity in H2 19.
3. Learn presentation skills by joining Toastmasters and participating in the program through the year.
4. Learn marketing by finding a mentor and complete 1 book bi-monthly as recommended by the mentor
5. Learn finance and engineering economics basics by the end of year.

Objectives:
1. Become a project manager by the end of 2020
2. Complete a DOT assignment in marketing
3. Start a graduate degree program

Slide 18

Now that we established how a career plan should look like, let's get into the details of building the activities based on the time periods.

> What are the specific considerations in developing the long-term activities in a career plan?

We start with planning the long-term activities first as these are closely related to the career vision that we just developed. Naturally, the conversation in the career advising session will transition from the vision to the long-term plan. For example, if you have a vison of becoming a general manager of a business group, I would then ask you, "what skill sets do you think a general manager need?" You may not know the exact answers as it is far in the future. To help you to develop this list, I often ask another question "Imagine that you were the general manager, what duties do you need to perform?" From this list of duties, we then look at the skills needed for each to develop a preliminary skills requirement list. The activities in obtaining these skills are your potential long-term activities, but don't put them in your career plan file yet. There are couple more steps to do.

Planning the Long-term Activities

- Develop your career vision
    - Envision the future and develop a list of duties
    - Generate a skills list for performing the duties

- Identify actionable activities to confirm your vision
    - Activities for confirming required duties and skills
    - Activities for defining the scope of the skills
    - Activities for developing the skill acquisition plan
    - Activities for identifying options and backups

- Exploit and trim the long-term activity list but keep the dropped activities for mid-term and short-term considerations

Slide 19

Since these activities are far in the future, they may not be totally clear to you at this time. Some may not be achievable for some reasons or you may not enjoy them when you find out what exactly is involved. However, you should not wait until the time comes to start getting into the details as it may be too late to achieve them or to change your career direction at that time. So, it is not wise to just write them down and table them until the future comes. You need to find out about these activities as much as possible and as early as possible. That means you should continue to develop a list of executable action items based on your long-term activity list. The purpose is to explore and confirm your career vision. Keep in mind that these actions are pathfinding in nature and not a comprehensive study of the areas. They are actually short-term and mid-term activities and we will discuss these in more detail when we plan activities for those periods. These action items should be small and can be executed between now and the beginning of the long-term period.

The first set of actions are to confirm the list of duties and the skills requirement list and to see if there are any items missing. These activities may include online researching on general manager job descriptions and LinkedIn profiles of people with general manager titles. It should also include face-to-face in person information gathering such as interviewing a general manager who you personally know, or your mentor can connect you with one. We can also look into attending networking events where general managers and HR professionals are present. You also need to find out good and bad things of the job from the people who have first-hand experiences. Job shadowing is a great way to see a job in action if opportunities are available.

The next set of actions are to understand the scope of the skills required for the job. We typically list the skills in general terms, such as communication, leadership, bioengineering, mathematics, finance, etc. There are a wide range of knowledge within these areas and one could pursue a Ph.D. degree in almost any of them. You must explore each subject matter in further detail to find out the level of the skills you need to obtain. The intention is to create a framework and for you to obtain a bigger picture of the requirements.

While exploring the skill scope requirements, you should also think about the potential ways to acquire these skills. Similarly, these activities are small and at a very high level. Examples are finding out if your company offers training classes, checking if a local university has open courses, and searching if there are good books written in the subjects. These activities may result in a high-level acquisition plan for the skills.

The last set of actions is related to creating options and backup plans as the future may be different from what we envision now. We need to be flexible and we sometimes may plan a dual-career path, which I have done by planning progressions in both industry and academia. Are there different paths to get to your vision? Is there a short path and a long path or even a dual path? What are the advantages and risks of each path? If your dream job is not realized as the way you imagined, what is your backup job? Could the skills that you are planning to obtain open up new areas and new opportunities? The activities in this last set are intended to answer the above questions and others in similar context.

While developing the four sets of path-finding activities, you can correlate them to the long-term activity list that we generated earlier. Through this exercise of developing the path-finding activities, you will find that certain long-term activities are related to common skills needed for most jobs. You need to move them out of the long-term activity list because you must improve them to have a good career anyway. These activities belong to the mid-term and short-term lists and we will use them later. This is one of the reasons why we start with the career plan with identifying long-term activities first. Another way to examine the list is through the degree of certainty. The items that you are certain to do, and you know the details should be in the list. All the fuzz items should not be on the long-term activity list until they are confirmed through the path-finding exploratory activities. By all means, the list is not final, and it needs to be updated regularly.

> What are the specific considerations in developing the mid-term activities in a career plan?

While the long-term career plan is tailored towards your vision – the peak career position, the mid-term career plan is designed for your next major career advancement, which is the next step towards your ultimate career objective. I typically start by asking the advisee "what is your next desired job position?" Most people can answer this question with a better degree of certainty compared to the long-term targeted position. As an advisor, I just need to make sure the desired position is aligned with the advisee's long-term vision and that upcoming career advancement objective can be a steppingstone leading to the ultimate career vision.

Next, I ask, "when do you think you will get that job?" The answer to this question varies since everyone has a different timeline, and this depends on the individual's time in current position and the aggressiveness of the individual's desires towards career advancement. It also depends on the industry you are in. In tech, for instance, people typically change jobs every two years. I suggest the rough timeline for mid-term activities is about one to three years. If your answer is longer, we need to find an achievable objective within this timeframe because it is too lax that you may lose focus and cadence and also difficult to plan specific activities when the time is too far in the future. It is perfectly fine to do a job longer, but you still need to set a career advancement objective within the next 1-3 years, which may be advancing to the next grade level or achieving a higher performance level that prepares you to move up a grade or change jobs.

Planning the Mid-term Activities

- Determine the next career advancement objective and the targeted achievable timeline
    - Next job position
    - Higher grade level or higher performance level

- Identify actionable activities for obtaining the next advancement
    - Obtaining the technical skills
    - Obtaining the 21st-century skills
    - Connecting to the opportunity

- Prioritize the mid-term activities

Slide 20

After the mid-term objective is identified, the next step is to determine the activities needed to achieve this objective. Unlike the long-term activities which may require exploring and pathfinding, mid-term activities are result and goal oriented. Actually, the short-term activities are similar in this perspective but serving different purpose, which we will discuss shortly. When defining these activities, they need to be explicit with SMART goals. SMART goal setting technique was coined by George Doran in 1981 and later modified by many others using different words to make up the acronym SMART [6]. The original five words were Specific, Measurable, Assignable, Realistic and Time-related.

To help identifying the mid-term activities, we can look from three major categories: activities needed for obtaining the technical skills, the 21st-century skills and connections to the advancement opportunity. The term "21st-century skills" replaced "soft skills" around the beginning of the century. It refers to core competencies that required for individuals to thrive in the current workplace, such as critical thinking, leadership, communication, problem-solving, negotiation, etc.

Improvements of the technical and 21st-century skills are associated with the "T" circle in the TOP model. For you to land your next position, you must connect your "T" circle to the "O" circle. Hence, you also need to identify ways to increase your connections to the opportunity, which takes time and planning as well. We will discuss the effective methods in greater details in the Session 5, Managing Your Environment.

At this planning stage, you can brainstorm the activities in three main areas. The first one is networking with the right people. Examples are attending industry seminars and professional conferences, finding mentors and connecting people through social media, LinkedIn and email. The second group of activities are related to self-promoting, such as building an accessible professional online profile. The last one would be job market researching, which includes online searching job opportunities and attending job fairs.

We should also review the activities that we came up in long-term career planning. We did the scale down the long-term list and some activities did not make the list. Now we can check to see if any of those activities enables you to meet your mid-term objectives. After we have a comprehensive list of activities, the last step is to prioritize the list. It would be best to have all activities in a ranking order but sometimes it is difficult to determine the exact order for a few activities, so we should at least prioritize the list into rank groups, such as in groups of very high, high, average, low, and very low priority. We will not remove any activities from the mid-term list. You will execute them based on priority. You may feel that you don't have time to do all of them in the timeline you set. It is ok at this stage and we will discuss how to make time in the next session to help you complete the list. The list is not final, and we may need to make some adjustments to have some of these activities starting in the short-term range. We will determine that when we plan the short-term activities.

> What are the specific considerations in developing the short-term activities in a career plan?

Now we are moving to planning the last group of activities, which are short-term activities. When we developed the long-term activity list, we already generated some path-finding activities for confirming your vision. These activities need to be done in the short-term and mid-term periods, but they are at a lower priority. One of the popular statements from advisees in career advising conversations is that they claim they are swamped with their current job and cannot spend much time and effort in planning and acquiring skills for the future. If a person needs work overtime constantly to meet the requirements of the current job after the probationary period, that means he or she may not be qualifying for the job. It is okay to work overtime once in a while as workload may not be linear and it is also fine that you are working overtime for additional responsibilities that leads to promotion or new opportunities. In short, you need to be successful at your current job with normal investment of time and effort before taking on the next advancement in your career. Improving your skills and the way you work so that you can do you current job easily and comfortably is the primary purpose of the short-term activities.

Planning the Short-term Activities

- Recognize the improvement areas on your current job. You may start by asking feedback from your manager, your peers, your client and customer

- Identify actionable activities to improve the performance of your current job in the areas:
    - Time – finish things quicker
    - Quality – get better results
    - Processes and methods – achieve better control and consistency, swap or hand off tasks to others who are better suited

- Consolidate and finalize the short-term plan

Slide 21

To start the process of identifying these short-term activities, I ask the advisee: "What are the things that you can improve to help you be more efficient in your current job?" If you don't know where to start, I suggest that you go ask feedback from your manager, your peers, and your clients and customers. We can also brainstorm from three areas: time, quality and processes. What can you do to finish your tasks sooner, getting better results, and having better control and consistency on the way you do things? The improvements activities make up your short-term critical activity list and they are often specific to your job.

I would like to see you utilize these improvements so that you can be successful at your current job before moving to your next job. Changing jobs because of failing at the current job is usually not the right approach in career development. In cases where an individual is not performing well at the current job and looking for a complete makeover of his or her career, the individual still needs to identify the root causes of the issues and take corrective actions to prevent them from happening again in the future. Therefore, addressing issues and improving the situation of your current job have higher priority over finding your next job and career vision. You need to take actions as soon as possible, hopefully tomorrow, to get you into a successful state, starting with the activity that has the most impact. Thus, your short-term critical activity list should be ranked in priority order. We will discuss the details on prioritization in Session 4, Managing Your Tasks.

> How to consolidate activities and present them as one career plan?

After developing the short-term critical activity list, we can compare it to the mid-term activity list. There may be duplicates or slight variations among the two lists. Also, some activities may be subsets of the others. We need to consolidate those activities and they will be treated as short-term critical activities. We may also find mid-term activities that are not similar to any short-term critical activity, but they can help to improve your current job, so we can start them earlier in the short-term. If there are mid-term activities targeted for your next job, but they require a long time to complete, such as getting an MBA degree, you may need to start them in the short-term or you won't be able to finish before your mid-term timeline. After adjusting the midterm activities into the short-term, we pull the path-finding activities that we generated in long-term plan and add them to the short-term activity list. However, these activities are at a lower priority.

Session 2 Summary: Developing a Career Plan

- Develop your career vision. It will be the North Star for all your career pursuits
- Map out the skill requirements for your vision and check to confirm their validity and feasibility
- Identify your next job and advancement as a mid-term objective and what you need to do to get it
- Seek improvement opportunities on your current job and take actions immediately
- The actions needed for improving your current job, obtaining your next job and achieving your vision make up your short, mid, and long-term career plan

Slide 22

The last step is entering all the activities in the Excel Career Planning Sheet shown in Page 27, Slide 18. The activities that has the highest priority, meaning the one you will do first, will be on the bottom row and the next one will be on the second bottom row and so on. These activities correlate with the learning axis and building your skills from the bottom to the top. You will highlight the cells to show the estimated execution time from the left to the right along with the time axis. When completing the sheet, you now have a baseline career development plan. You will need to update it as time passes and when your activities are progressing. I recommend that you should update it at least by quarter. Giving yourself a grade on the progress each quarter may keep you on track. Reviewing the plan and progress with your career advisor regularly can also help you to keep engaged.

Now that you have a career plan, you may feel overwhelmed by all the activities and wonder how to find time to execute the plan. It is a common concern, and it requires certain level of willpower to execute. You need to believe in yourself that you can do this. Knowing and mastering the execution techniques will help you to boost your confidence and will enable you to do it smoothly. We will transition the discussion to execution techniques starting with time management. The next session will help you to make time so that you can complete all these activities.

Session 2 Exercise – Develop a career plan

Step 1. The ultimate career vision

My career vision: (Ideal position at the peak of career)

Dream Job #1: _____

Backup or dual: _____

Time to achieve: _____

Step 2. Identify required skills. If there are not enough rows and spaces, do this on your own paper.

Duties to skills: (Skills needed for each major duty)

Major duty #1: _Ex: Budget forecast_

Required skills: _Finance, accounting, data analysis,_

tool skills: Crystal Ball and Excel

Major duty #2: _____

Required skills: _____

_____

Major duty #3: _____

Required skills: _____

_____

Major duty #4: _____

Required skills: _____

_____

Major duty #5: _____

Required skills: _____

_____

Step 3. Identify preliminary long-term activities

Rev.0 Long-term activities: (Actions to obtain the skills)

Skill	Activity

Step 4. Identify Path-finding activities for confirming long-term plan:

Activities for confirming required duties and skills

P1	
P2	
P3	

Activities for defining the scope of the skills

P4	
P5	
P6	

Activities for developing the skill acquisition plan	
P7	
P8	
P9	

Activities for identifying options and backups	
P10	
P11	
P12	

Step 5. Trim and reduce the Long-term activity list

#	Long-term Activity	Skill
L1		
L2		
L3		
L4		
L5		

Step 6. The next big career advancement milestone

My next job: (Targeted next job position)

My next position: _____

Backup or dual: _____

Time to achieve: _____
               If longer than 3 years, fill out the next box

My next progression: (Targeted next grade/performance level)
My next progression: _____
Backup or dual: _____
Time to achieve: _____
Should be less than 3 years

Step 7. Identify preliminary mid-term activities – actions needed to reach your next advancement milestone.

Activities for obtaining the technical skills

1. _____
2. _____
3. _____
4. _____

Activities for obtaining the 21st-century skills

5. _____
6. _____
7. _____
8. _____

Activities for connecting to the opportunity

9. _____
10. _____
11. _____

Step 8. Prioritize the mid-term activity list (feel free to adjust priority)

#	Mid-term Activity	Priority
M1		High
M2		
M3		
M4		
M5		
M6		Average
M7		
M8		
M9		
M10		
M11		Low

Step 9. Identify short-term activities - to do things quicker and better

#	Short-term Critical Activity	Impact
S1		High
S2		
S3		
S4		
S5		
S6		
S7		
S8		
S9		Low

Step 10. Consolidate and finalize the baseline career plan by inputting Long-term activities (L#), mid-term activity (M#), short-term activities (L#) and path-finding activities (P#)

Vision:

Target Date: 2023

Knowledge Areas	Jan19	Feb19	Mar19	Apr19	May19	Jun19	Jul19	Aug19	Sep19	Oct19	Nov19	Dec19	Q1 20	Q2 20	Q3 20	Q4 20	2021	2022	2023
Skill 11									P2	P4	P5	P7		P9	P10	P12	L2	L4	L5
Skill 10								P1		P3		P6		P8		P11	L1	L3	
Skill 9															M10	M11			
Skill 8														M6	M9				
Skill 7																			
Skill 6						M1							M4	M5					
Skill 5									S8										
Skill 4					S5			S7					M3		M8				
Skill 3			S3																
Skill 2		S2		S4			S6				S9		M2		M7				
Skill 1	S1																		
Time	Jan19	Feb19	Mar19	Apr19	May19	Jun19	Jul19	Aug19	Sep19	Oct19	Nov19	Dec19	Q1 20	Q2 20	Q3 20	Q4 20	2021	2022	2023

Goals: 1. Time: _____

2. Quality: _____

3. Process and Methods: _____

Objectives: Become _____ by _____

Session 3

Managing Your Time

Make time

> ## Session 3: Managing Your Time
>
> Time is the scarcest resource, thus time management is the most critical and fundamental skill
>
> *Understand bad behaviors*
> - Avoid bad habits and build good ones
>
> *Understand your time*
> - How much time do you have?
>
> *Make time*
> - "It's not about 'having' time. It's about making time."
>   - Anonymous
>
> Slide 24

> Why is time management so important?

Many people claim that they are so busy with their current job and living routines, leaving them no time for future career development. It sounds like an excuse but is a common reason why people are not actively engaging in career development. In my opinion, time is the scarcest resource for all of us. Our lifetime is short, and we only live once. Once time passes, we will never get it back. On the other hand, everyone has the same amount of time in a day, a week, a month and a year. People who manage time well will be able to accomplish more than those who don't. Time management is the first skill that I recommend advisees to obtain among all skills. For some advisees, I actually started with this session before developing career plans because they stated that they were busy and had concerns about spending time on career development.

Mainstream Time Management Tips

- Focus on planning
    - Make a to-do list
    - Prioritize – based on urgency and importance
    - Organize – calendar, reminders, deadlines, etc.
    - Create a schedule – daily plan, weekly plan, etc.

  Life is never going the way we planned. Plan and re-plan take time away from actual execution

- Assume an individual is in the position to
    - Say no
    - Delegate
    - Block off time

  May not be suitable for people in early career

Slide 25

What are the common drawbacks in mainstream time management methods?

Searching the web, there are many techniques and tips in time management. They typically involve making a to-do list, prioritizing based on urgency and importance, keeping things organized and creating a schedule. These are mostly planning activities. I found that many people spend a lot of time on doing the time management plan, but life is never going the way we planned. When new priorities or interruptions occur, people have to forgo the plan or spend more time to modify the plan, which is an oxymoron as such time management activities actually waste your time. It is not uncommon that people eventually give up doing the schedule and just react to what the lives take them. Having a plan has benefits but keep in mind that the plan is merely your wish on a piece of paper. The most important part of time management is what you actually do and how you act and react in real time situations but not what you plan you should do.

There are also general recommendations such as to say no, delegate and block off your time, which are fine only if you are in the position to do so. People at the beginning of their career often cannot say no to people and have no one to delegate tasks. These advices give the impression that time management skill is for managers and executives, and they are tailored to management and senior leaders who are more pressed in time. I believe that everyone's time is equally valuable to that individual, and an individual should not wait until getting into management to focus on time management. In fact, time management skill is even more critical for entry level employees as they have less control over their environments. They have less options and resources to make time for themselves, and many of them cannot move up because they have to keep doing the busy work. They need a time management system that can help them to get out of the busy routine and make time to grow their skills and career.

I am about to introduce you an uncommon time management method that I devised and practice. It has helped me to manage my time effectively and achieved good results in my dual careers in high-tech and academia. By the way, I don't do a schedule with the exception of doing projects required at work. I do minimal planning for my time and put the time in actual execution. I have to put a disclaimer here that my method may not be suitable for everyone due to personality differences, but I strongly believe that it can be adopted by most people. Nothing is perfect for everyone in this world. You have to practice it situationally and modify it to suit your case. When you first adopt the method, it requires a couple exercises at the beginning, so you do have to put in some administrative time, but you will gain a lot more time back after you use the method. The essence of my method is simply changing behaviors and setting general guidance for activities, after that it is all about execution.

Introducing a New Time Management Practice

- Minimal planning and emphasis on execution
- Less effort on administration; more action oriented
- Main focus of the method
    - Change behaviors
    - Understand the nature of your activities
    - Set general guiding principles
    - Execute and act under these principles
- Adoption
    - To aid adoption use the exercises at first
    - Practice the method and modify to suit your situation

Slide 26

What are the bad behaviors to avoid in time management?

Before I get into the details of using my system, we need to be aware of the bad behaviors in time management. The first bad behavior is procrastination, which is exemplified by the student syndrome shown on Slide #27. Throughout years of education, from grade school to college, most people are accustomed to homework and exam deadlines and thus develop the habit of pacing their effort until the deadline is near as indicated in the graph on the next page. Since students are not experts in the subject being studied, they do not have total control over the plan which results in missed deadlines. Such habits are carried over into the workplace where there is little control over the plan that resulted in their assigned tasks and its associated deadlines.

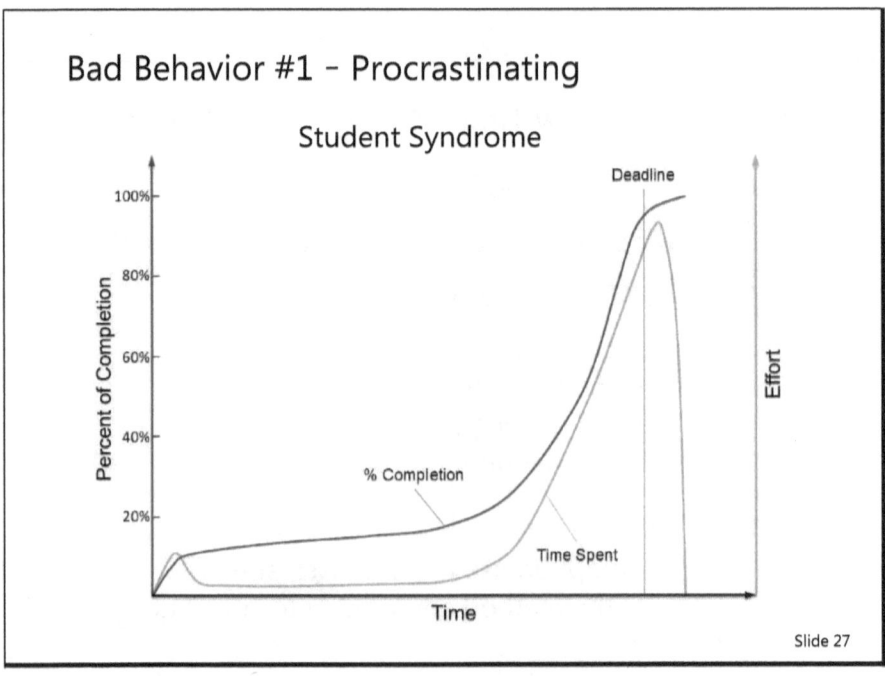

Scheduling a task with a deadline also leads to another bad behavior padding, which is adding safety buffer when determining the task duration to allow the task to be done by the deadline with comfortable degree of confidence. When people estimate task durations to set deadlines in scheduling, they tend to provide the estimated time between 70% and 90% certainty of completion. Of course, this also depends on the personality of the individual; some people are more conservative and only committed to what they can deliver, while others are more optimistic and willing to take risks. Most people would not be comfortable in using the 50% mean average, as there is still a 50-50 chance of missing the deadline, and people typically want to have a higher success rate than a coin-toss probability.

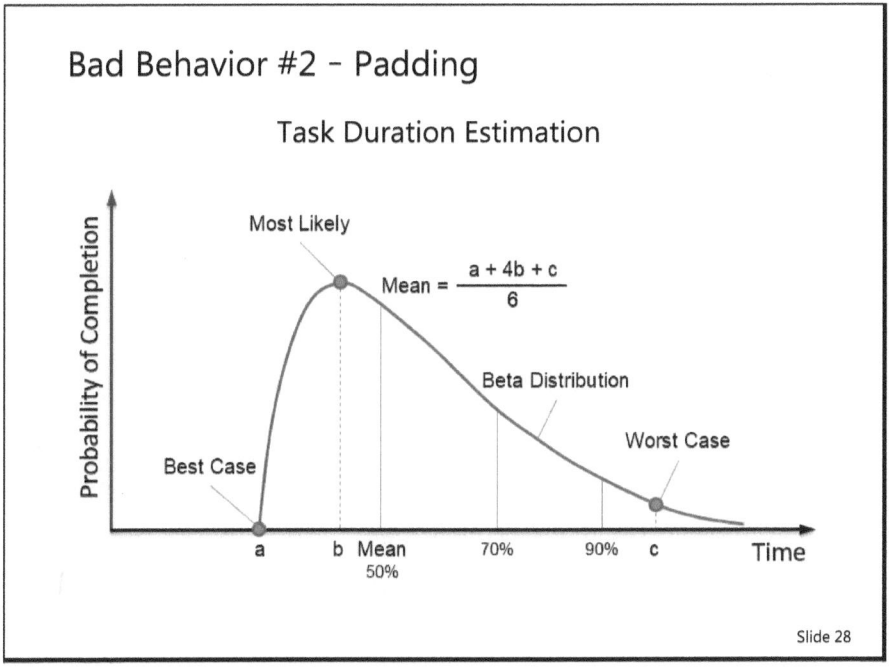

It is well known that the probability of a task completion is best represented by the Beta distribution as shown on Slide #28. This distribution is commonly used for task time estimates in project management. Time "a" is the best-case scenario for completing a task, whereas time "b" is the most likely completion time and time "c" is the worst-case scenario when most things go wrong. The mean can be calculated as (a+4b+c)/6, where there is a 50% chance for the task to be completed. Even if an individual schedules a task using the mean duration, there is still a small buffer between the mean and the "most likely" completion point. In other words, statistically, this task is likely to be completed sooner than the mean time. If you push yourself further aiming for the best case, you can certainly finish the task even earlier. However, most people manage their time by setting a schedule with task deadlines, and the deadlines that they typically use are far more conservative than the mean completion time. Clearly, a schedule with task deadlines is filled with padding. Setting such deadlines actually alters the statistical nature of the task duration. According to Parkinson's Law, "work expands so as to fill the time available for its completion" [7]. By setting a deadline with padding, you give yourself a comfort zone to finish the task, but at the same time, you also give yourself an excuse to procrastinate, believing that you are effective as long as you follow the schedule and complete the tasks before the deadlines.

Some people may argue that we can set the deadlines but do the tasks as fast as possible in actual execution. Well, if that is the case, why do we have a schedule knowing that we are not going to follow the schedule. Why do we waste time to plan the work but not follow the plan? Some people may suggest that we set deadlines based on the best-case time or the most likely time, so that we can push ourselves to be more effective in finishing tasks in a timely manner. By doing this, you have to face a higher failure rate in executing to your schedule, which means your schedule is likely to change, and you have to spend time to modify and keep it valid.

The main purpose of a deadline is to measure our performance in managing time. We feel good when we meet the deadline and feel bad when we miss it. This feeling has been enforced by our parents when we are young, by our teachers when we are at school, and by our bosses and co-workers when we are at work. Therefore, as long as there are deadlines for tasks in a schedule, people will put padding into time estimates to ensure their success and avoid feeling bad. However, it is a false sense of success because you are not really effective when you meet the deadlines and complete a schedule with padding. You can and you should do better than that.

The cause for padding is due to the concern of risks and interruptions. Interruptions are often a result of multitasking, which is the third bad practice in time management. Many managers believe that employees should develop the ability to handle multiple tasks, so it is common to see multitasking as a requirement in job descriptions. It is fine to require employees to learn and cover multiple areas, but that does not mean multitasking. True multitasking rarely happens, as most people cannot do two things at once. A typical task execution scenario with and without multitasking is shown on Slide #29.

Multitasking means switching from task to task and switching from one task to another is basically an interruption. While the total time required for both tasks remains the same in both cases, the time required to finish Task 1 is extended with multitasking. What really matters is when a task is completed. Therefore, it is obvious that focusing on finishing one task at a time yields a better result.

The illustration does not account for the inefficiency of switching between tasks. In reality, when we are switching from one task to another, it typically requires a ramping period for us to get back into focus, so the situation is worse than shown. A similar situation occurs in production where equipment is dedicated to specific products as much as possible to minimize setup and switching time. In manufacturing, production schedules are generally more succinct, compressed and visual compared to project schedules. The Lean philosophy with continuous waste elimination contributes to these characteristics of production schedules. Many of the Lean practices can be applied to time management, and you will see these in the design of my time management system shortly.

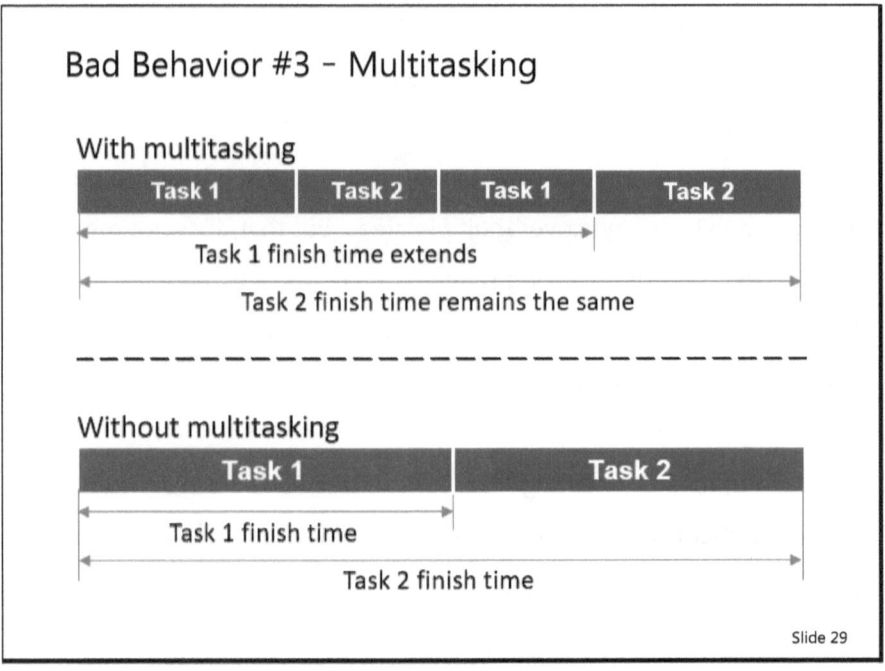

To achieve better time management in task execution, you must be willing to change the bad behaviors in time management, which means avoiding or reducing procrastination, padding and multitasking as much as possible. Practicing the new time management method that I proposed will help you to make these changes in your behaviors to make time. Following this method, you do not need a schedule, and of course there are no deadlines either, but it doesn't mean you don't need to plan your activities. You need a prioritized task list and then just execute the tasks one by one with focus. It sounds simple and I believe it is, but you need to change your attitude and behavior first.

> Do you know how you spend time and why is it important for you to know?

To set you up for adopting the new time management method, you need to know how you spend your time. This is similar to managing your finances. You will not be effective if you don't know how you spend your money. Understanding how you spend your time will help you to identify waste and inefficiencies. There is a more important purpose, which is helping you to build a positive can-do attitude for taking on challenging tasks.

As I mentioned previously, the most common excuse I have heard in career mentoring sessions is that "I am very busy now and don't have time for development." I respond by taking these people through an exercise to help them understand their time. I will demonstrate this exercise based on my own calculations, and you can apply the same logic to your situation and do this using the template provided in the exercise section at the end of this session.

The exercise is based on a typical workweek:
- There are **168** hours in a week.
- I typically work five 8-hour days, but I am adding an extra day per week. That is 48 hours. I live close by work, so this includes commute. I have **120** hours left.

- I need to sleep and the recommended sleep time for adults is 7 hours per day (6 hours may already be appropriate typically and that is actually my average). To be more conservative, I use the total of 49 hours. I have **71** hours left.
- I eat 3 meals a day and let's use half an hour per meal average. Dinners may take longer but breakfasts are typically shorter. The total eating time is 10.5 hours. I have **60.5** hours left.
- For personal hygiene, I put 1 hour per day. Total 7 hours. I have **53.5** hours left.
- I want to stay healthy, so I need to exercise. The Department of Health and Human Services recommends 30 minutes exercise per day for healthy adults. That is 3.5 hours. I have **50** hours left.

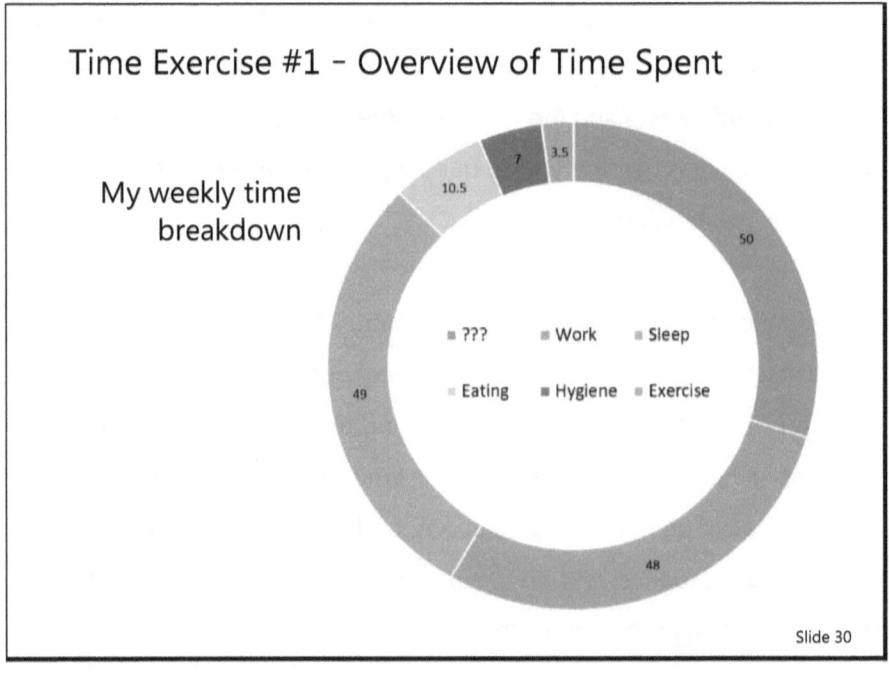

I am stopping the calculation here and the percentage breakdown of my time is shown on Slide #30. Clearly, I have a significant amount of time left, 50 hours, which is an amount greater than any of the activities I have just listed. The calculation does not include excursions, nor does not include vacation and holidays either. Of course, there are some weeks when I spend more time in some categories, but statistically, it offers a good representation in the long run.

I had started working full time before I decided to pursue a doctorate degree. As most people know, doctorate degrees typically require studying full-time, and pursuing such a degree is a significant commitment. In the book *Outliers*, Malcolm Gladwell repeatedly mentioned the "10,000 Hour Rule," which is the time it takes to become an expert in a field. That is about 38.5 hours per week for five years, which is the typical duration for a doctorate program. At the time, I did the above calculations. With the 38.5 hours deduced, I still had 11.5 hours left. I figured that my sleep time calculation was conservative, and I could also negotiate with my manager to fit my work within 40 hours. Plus, I had 3 weeks of vacation and 11 days of holidays. So, I convinced myself that it was doable, and I did it, not just once. I earned doctorate degrees in engineering and business and received three doctorate degree certificates. After that, I use the time to teach, at least 2 courses per term, staying in school.

As you can see, this exercise played a significant role in my decision to take on a significant endeavor on top of my full-time job, and this decision resulted in my attitude change, giving me the confidence to do even more. There was a period when I was studying in the doctorate program, teaching, working and also having a newborn child at home. By the way, I did not sacrifice my work performance at all. I had "Exceed" and "outstanding" rating in most of the annual performance reviews. The most valuable lesson I learned was how to make time through this process.

I encourage you to do the calculations and understand where your time goes. You can follow what I did and may continue to include other activities such as family time, socializing with friends, commute, etc. When you are done, I bet that you will still have a considerably large amount of time that is not accounted for. Then, the question is what are you going to do with this time? I hope your answer is improving your skills for career development. If you do decide to pursue an advanced degree, Session 6 may help you as it contains my learning from all these years in school. Knowing you have extra time and determining to take on a challenge are not enough; you need to make time to become effective. "It's not about 'having' time. It's about making time."

> How to make time?

We will do another exercise to explain how to make time. Before we start, I want to share the background of this exercise. There is a management philosophy called Lean, which is a concept that grew out of the Toyota Production System. It is aiming at improving manufacturing efficiency through waste elimination. In the Lean tool kit, there is one tool called Value Stream Mapping (VSM). Unconventionally, I apply the VSM concept in time management.

VSM is a Lean technique used to analyze a work process flow. Activities in the process flow are categorized as either value-adding, necessary waste or waste. The goal is to build a future state process with the least amount of waste. This is typically done in a team environment using Post-it notes to represent activities and then mapping the current process state on a board. Data for each activity, such as process time, inventory, materials and quality requirements are also captured. Then each activity is analyzed and categorized using colored stickers on the Post-it notes with green for value-adding, red for waste and yellow for necessary waste. Finally, redesign the process flow by removing or reducing waste and necessary waste.

We start the exercise by picking a typical workday to apply VSM. First, starting with a time in the day, for instance, the time you get up in the morning. And then one after another, list all the typical activities and their durations. Next categorize the activities and color code them, green for value-adding activities, yellow for enabling activities and red for all the rest. For example, working time is green as you earn a salary. Sleep time is yellow but only up to the recommended hours and any additional sleep time is red. The same logic applies to eating, hygiene and exercise. If you feel that certain family time is very important, put it as green. After you finish the category assignments, you can calculate the percentages of each category. When you complete this for a workday, do the same for an off-day.

You now know how efficient you are in utilizing your time and where your time is wasted. After you understand your current state, you can plan a typical workday and an off-day for the future state. The purpose of doing this is not to schedule your life like a machine so that you don't have any fun. First, it gives you an overall target for the day, whether is a workday or an off-day. When you get up in the morning, you have a goal to achieve, and when the day ends, you know your performance of the day. Second, it makes you conscious of your time, so at any given moment, you know if you are doing green, red or yellow. If you are doing red, try to hurry up and shift to yellow or green.

For instance, you may be out to have a drink with your friends but instead of staying there for 3 hours, cutting it down to 2 hours. It would not hurt your friendship and you save an hour for green activities.

By associating your activities with colors, you know what to prioritize quickly. More importantly, you know if you are doing good or bad at any time. It enables you make decision quickly and in real time, which change your behavior in utilizing time. It also allows you to plan your time better by combining green activities with red or yellow activities, such as allocating some meal time to socializing with friends, co-worker and your mentors. When you have high priority activities or excursions, you will also know where to make time available. Another side benefit of this method is pushing you into a better life routine, sleeping when you should, getting up on time daily, and having a meal when you are supposed to eat, which results in another behavior change.

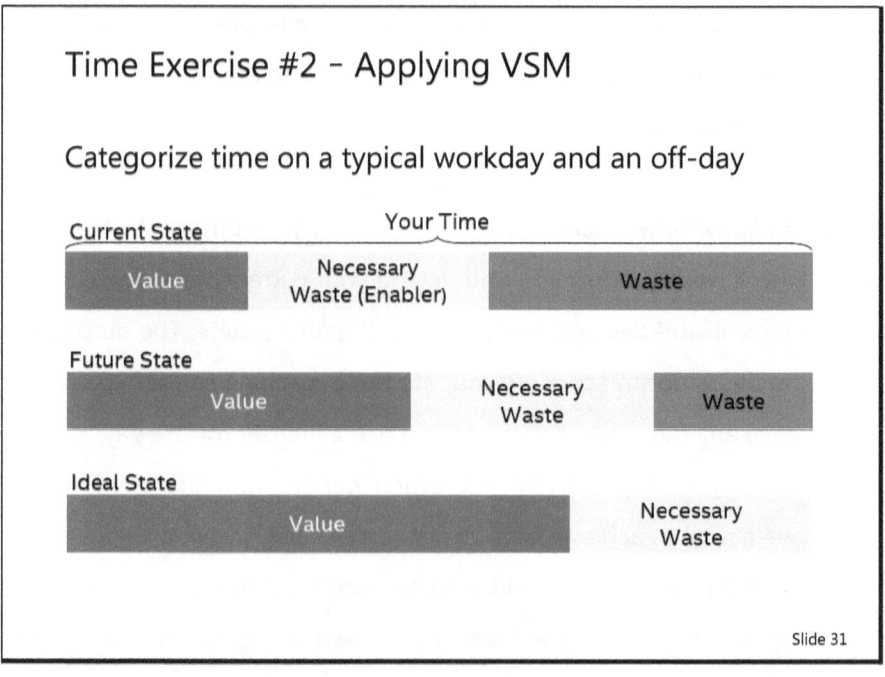

As shown on Slide #31, the ideal state is to eliminate all red activities. It is the ultimate goal but nearly impossible to achieve. It is fine to have waste remaining, but your future state must have improvements over the current state. The red activities are your first focus. There are numerous ways to set your goal for the future state. You can roughly track your time by percentage breakdown and set a goal for reducing certain percentage of red by week, by month or by quarter. You can also set targets for reaching certain percentage of green or red. When you are achieving your goal and feel that you cannot eliminate any more reds, you can move on to optimize the yellow activities. You may be able to turn some yellows into greens, e.g. taking public transportation and reading a book so your commute time is no longer all yellow.

You can further optimize your green time as well. I also apply this unconventional application of VSM in time management to my time at work. To me, this time is already a value-adding activity as I earn a salary in return, but not all activities that I do at work create value for my company. Using VSM, you can do the same analysis to your work hours, and waste can be identified and removed as well. You can use the time saved to improve your skills, which benefits you, but since it also improves your work performance, your company should not mind. Now you double the benefit of this green time. Clearly, this can be used for personal time management in addition to work process improvement. It benefits both the company and you personally.

This time management method worked well for me and enabled me to achieve some substantial accomplishments. Most people think that I am much older than my actual age based on my biography - working full-time in high-tech for over 30 years, teaching part-time at universities for 20 years, earning multiple doctorate degrees, writing several books, having a family and raising two children, in addition to engaging in many hobbies and volunteering activities. This time management method enables me to live my life to the fullest. In other words, I have made a lot of time.

> What are the key points in practicing the unconventional time management method proposed in this book?

Practicing the New Time Management Method

- Complete the weekly time breakdown exercise
    - Know where your time goes
    - Set goals to utilize your unaccounted time
- Complete the VSM analysis for a typical workday and an off-day
    - Determine the color of your activities
    - Know the rough percentage of each color
- Set routine templates for a workday and an off-day
    - Follow the routine and build the habit
    - Focus on execution: avoid the red, do the green and optimize yellow and green activities

Slide 32

Adopting my method is simple, and the biggest effort is completing the two exercises that I just showed you. The first exercise helps to build confidence and motivation to take on challenges, which gives you the internal drive to pursue excellence and advancement. I hope this exercise gives you the can-do attitude towards the career development plan that you created in the last session. The second exercise maps your activities and imprints the associated color codes in your mind. I hope that from now on, you can identify the color for any activity, and in any moment of time, you are aware that if you are doing green, yellow or red. The executing principle is simple, avoid the red, do the green and optimize the yellow and green.

Practicing this method will change your behavior. At the beginning, as I mentioned earlier, you can track your time and see how well you do each day, but don't spend too much time to do that. Eventually, you need to put your time in execution and avoid administrative tasks which may be yellow but definitely not green. That is the reason why you need to create two targeted routines, one for a typical workday and one for an off-day. Getting into a better routine helps you track your time easier at the beginning, which will save your time as a result. In addition, it enables consistency in execution and helps to you to build the habit.

The bottom-line focus is execution. Which color of activity to engage in is your decision to make in real time, and you need to make the decision quickly. For example, if you are up a bit early in the morning, and there is not enough time to go back to sleep, you have a decision to make: lying in bed until your normal getup time or getting up to start your daily routine. Another example is when you finish a task early and have to wait for others to continue the next step. What would you do? In the mainstream time management practice where a schedule is used, you are not pressed to do anything because you are not late per the schedule. Life is filled with uncertainties and that is why we put buffers in our schedule. When uncertainties occur, which are more often than we think, we then feel the need to spend more time to plan thoroughly and put more safety buffers in the schedule. Do you see the problem with this approach? We are not only wasting more time to plan but also putting more waste in the plan. Whether or not there is a plan, or unplanned events happen to us, we should know what to do real time while we are executing, and my method offers a simple principle to follow.

Session 3 Summary: Managing Your Time

- Mainstream time management relies on setting and following a schedule with deadlines for activities
    - Promote bad behaviors: Procrastinating, padding and multitasking
    - Take time away from execution

- Introducing a new method focusing on behavior change and waste elimination
    - Understand your time and categorize activities
    - Build a positive attitude to take on challenges
    - Make time for value-added activities
    - Focus on execution with a simple logic

Slide 33

When you have a list of things to do, scan it so that you can associate them with the color codes. Then just start to execute the green activities one at a time and avoid multitasking as much as possible. Multitasking often involves extra yellow activities, such as transitions from one task to another. When you have many green activities, which one should you do first? The answer to this question is the focus of the next session: Session 5, Managing Your Tasks.

Session 3 Exercise #1 - Identify your time

Step 1. Typical weekly time breakdown

Input activity time & calculate time remaining: (Start from 168 hours for a week minus time used)

Activity	Time Used	Time Remaining
Work	hours	hours
Sleep	hours	hours
Meals	hours	hours
Hygiene	hours	hours
Exercise	hours	hours
Family time	hours	hours
Social time	hours	hours
Commute	hours	hours
Learning/Classes	hours	hours
	hours	hours
	hours	hours
	hours	hours

Step 2. Utilize the unaccounted time

Unaccounted time: (Remaining time after all activities)

I have _____ hours left per week.

Tentatively, I can use the time to do the following:

#1 _____ Time used: _____ hours
Time Remaining: _____ hours

#2 _____ Time used: _____ hours
Time Remaining: _____ hours

#3 _____ Time used: _____ hours
Time Remaining: _____ hours

Session 3 Exercise #2 – Make time

Step 1. Apply VSM to a typical workday

Current workday: (Breakdown as detail as possible to 5 min.)

Start Time	Task	Time Used	Task Color
	Get up		
	Go to sleep		

Breakdown	Green	Yellow	Red
Time			
% Total			

Step 2. Apply VSM to a typical off-day

Current off-day: (Breakdown as detail as possible to 5 min.)

Start Time	Task	Time Used	Task Color
	Get up		
	Go to sleep		

Breakdown	Green	Yellow	Red
Time			
% Total			

Step 3. Set goals and develop a workday routine template

My goal for period _____ to _____:

My Target	Green	Yellow	Red
Time			0
% Total			0%

Workday routine template:

Start Time	Task	Time Used	Task Color
	Get up		
	Go to sleep		

Step 4. Set goals and develop an off-day routine template

My goal for period _____ to _____:

My Target	Green	Yellow	Red
Time			0
% Total			0%

Off-day routine template:

Start Time	Task	Time Used	Task Color
	Get up		
	Go to sleep		

Session 4

Managing Your Tasks

Achieve exceptional results

Session 4: Managing Your Tasks

You get results because you take actions to do things and do them right.

Prioritizing tasks
- "The first step to success is knowing your priorities." - Arpesh

Performing beyond expectations
- Not only doing things well but surprisingly well

Managing risks
- "Only those who risk going too far can possibly find out how far one can go." - T. S. Eliot

Slide 35

What is task management?

Task management in the context of this book is simply execution management. We get results because we execute tasks and to live a fulfilling life, we have many tasks to do. In Session#2, we generated your career plan. The more you do along with getting better results, the more accomplishments you achieve. If it is done right, your career plan should consist of an extensive list of tasks to complete. We showed you how to make time in Session#3, and now we are going to show you how to execute tasks effectively to get great results. There are three aspects to getting great results.

First, you need to decide what to do first, second and so on, which means determining the priority of the tasks. Second, you need to achieve exceptional results and not just simply get things done. Last, you need to push yourself to the edge of your limits to achieve great success, but it is also important to know how far is too far. We must take risks but informed risks and not foolish risks.

> What is the priority matrix method, and should you use it?

When searching online, the most popular prioritization method is to apply a matrix of importance and urgency. The recommendations are as follows:

1) Do the tasks now if they are important and urgent.
2) Do the tasks next if they are important but less urgent.
3) Do the tasks last if they are urgent but less important.
4) Don't do the tasks that are not important or urgent.

This method certainly helps when you initiate those tasks or know the details of these tasks. There are two major issues with this method. The first issue is assuming that you can determine the importance and urgency of the tasks. Many people, especially at the beginning of their career, have tasks assigned to them by their department manager, project managers and team members, and often everyone says that the tasks are high priority. Therefore, if you have little control over your environment, meaning you have to do what other people say, or you are new to the organization, this method does not work well.

The second issue of following this method is that by putting the urgent tasks first, you are building a habit of firefighting. If this method is practiced by everyone in an orgnization, people will most likely tell you their tasks are urgent in order to get you to do what they want you to do first. Sometimes, people even intentionally create an urgent situation so that everyone will prioritize it to get it done. There is a quote that people use to address this issue: "A lack of planning on your part does not constitute an emergency on my part." You don't want to be in a situation where you are constantly firefighting and forced to do everything due to urgency. In most cases, taking time to do a task without being hurried will produce a better quality result. Ideally, you should do things at your own pace and in the order that is based on realistic urgency and importance.

Prioritization is Situational

- How to prioritize tasks depends on how much control you have over your environment
- You have less situational control if
    - tasks are assigned to you rather than initiated by you
    - you are new to the organization or the project
    - you don't have enough information on the tasks
    - you have too many urgent tasks
- Priority matrix based on task importance and urgency is not effective when you have less situational control
- Prioritize based on estimated completion time

Slide 36

Obviously, prioritization is situational. The priority matrix method will not work if you don't have much control over your environment. For instance, your boss may come to you and assign several tasks for you to complete this week. Which one should you do first? The straightforward way would be ask your manager to provide you the priority, but I caution you not to do this often. It is okay only when you are new to the organization or your manager. If you are doing this too often, your manager would think that you are not independent and require too much handholding and supervision. Therefore, eventually, you need to determine the priority on your own. If you use the priority matrix method, you need to know how important and urgent these tasks are. Likewise, you should not rely on your manager for this information as this would take too much time for your manager to explain. Again, you need to determine the importance and urgency of these tasks on your own.

In addition to tasks from your manager, you may also get tasks from your team or other project managers in the organization. You need to evaluate the tasks to determine their importance and urgency, but you will often find the priority is different based on the individual involved and based on different individual perspectives. You may prioritize tasks by either putting the company first, your manager first, or your team first. However, doing the right things for your company may not mean it is right for your manager or your team, and vice versa. When you have many assigned tasks and are told that they are all high priority, it does not matter how you prioritize them, you will not be able to please everyone. Most people start their career in this situation. Hence, I am introducing a simple method to help you prioritize your tasks.

> What is the time-based prioritization method, and when should it be used?

This method is prioritizing the tasks based on estimated task completion time. We will use a specific example to demonstrate how this method works. Let's say you are assigned several tasks by management this week. You are told that they are all important. When you list them and estimate the time to complete each task, you find that the total time exceeds your work time, which is typical because your organization hires you to produce the maximum output. Most managers do not want you to have free time. In other words, they typically overload you with work with the intent of maximizing people resources.

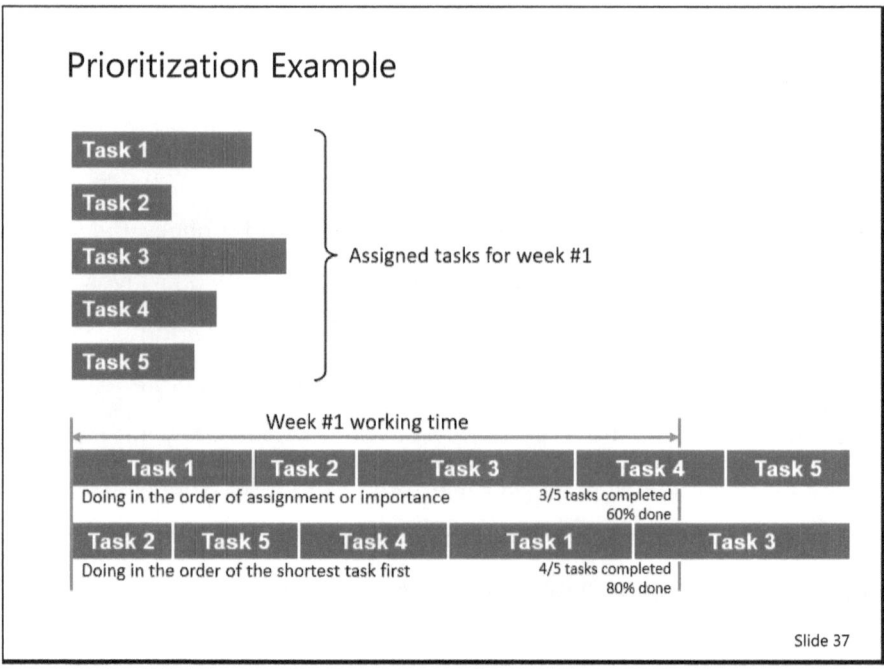

As shown on Slide #37, when you prioritize tasks in the order assigned to you or use the priority matrix, you will complete 3 of the 5 tasks. If the tasks are prioritized according to the estimated completion time, the shortest task is executed first, then the next shortest task is executed, and so on, resulting in completing 4 out of 5 tasks. What matters to management is task completion, not the time you spend on a particular task. As a result, your performance is usually measured by the number of tasks completed, not by hours worked. In addition, working on the shorter tasks allows you to get experience and acquire skills faster and become more valuable to the company. Also, shorter tasks are less likely to be blocked by an obstacle or impediment or waiting on feedback from your manager, resulting in less context switching and overhead is going between multiple tasks that are work in process.

There is a task, Task #3, that is left unfinished by the end of the week. Will you continue to finish this task in the following week? The answer is yes but only up to the time when new tasks are assigned to you again. At such time, you need to evaluate the new tasks and start fresh with the same principle of doing the shortest tasks first. This is demonstrated on Slide #38.

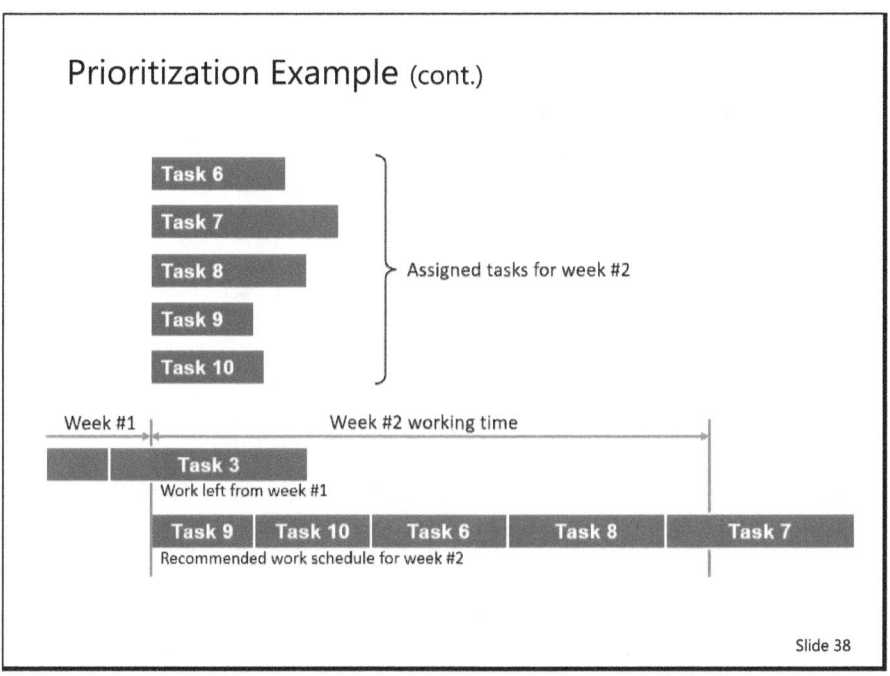

You may be wondering what happened to Task #3. Yes. Don't worry about Task #3 if your manager did not mention it in the last meeting. The reason is that things and priorities often change at work, especially if you are working in a dynamic environment. Whatever things on your manager's mind are his or her biggest worries and largest needs. In other words, the tasks your manager asked you to perform at that time were considered priorities. Since these are important and urgent, your manager would have told others, not just depended on you.

When you are new or have less situational control in your work environment, there is a very high probability that the issues may have already been solved by others. Also, longer tasks are often more complex, and you cannot compete with your peers to solve them quickly when you are new. In addition, longer tasks often have more unknowns and by the time you get around to working on that longer task, it is likely that some of the unknowns will have been figured out by other tasks that have been worked on by you or other team members. To add value to your team, you should focus on making quick turnaround rather than solving difficult tasks. Therefore, the method of doing the shortest task first allows you to have a chance to complete some tasks before your peers, so you are seen as a contributing member of the team.

As your career progresses and you become a senior employee on your team, should you no longer use this method? The answer is no, and this method still applies. The higher your position, the more strategic it is. You will be often asked to develop experimental proposals with higher uncertainties. It is possible that your manager quickly realizes what he or she asked you to experiment is not a smart idea or a viable solution.

Would your manager come to you and admit that it was a mistake and you don't need to do it anymore? Most likely not as it may consider losing face or undermine his or her credibility and authority. Often, your manager lets you continue finishing the proposal and even praises you after it is done, but the proposal is filed in a drawer without seeing any daylight.

In both cases, whether you are new or senior, it is human nature that people will seek you out when they want you to do things, but they will not necessarily make an effort to tell you when these tasks are no longer needed. Using the proposed time-based prioritization method can minimize waste in your time investment. You will find that there are many tasks you won't need to finish. What if your manager comes to you and ask about Task #3 again within the week? Quite simply, you now know it is a priority and should get back to it immediately. Whenever you are assigned new tasks or reminded of previous tasks, you need to reset your task prioritization. This method can be used as long as tasks are assigned to you.

Some people may find this a cunning way to avoid work and play politics with management. As a manager who frequently assigns tasks to my employees, I actually prefer this method when there is an open understanding in my team. My team focuses on making quick turns and taking action on the tasks immediately after assigned. They do not need to waste their time and my time checking with me on tasks assigned previously. As long as I am not asking about these tasks again, they do not need to do them, since it may be due to new strategy changes, my mistakes or faster completion by others. In some cases, I can assign multiple people the same task to solve an urgent issue independently without worrying about wasting too much of everyone's time, and I am certain that it will be resolved in the fastest time possible.

> What are the pros and cons of the time-based prioritization method?

Obviously, the time-based prioritization method promotes fast action by maximizing the highest percentage of tasks completed in a given period of time. In the case shown on Slide #37, 80% of the tasks have been completed instead of 60%. Getting results faster and completing more tasks will increase your reputation among managers and teams. For those focused on unfinished tasks, you are more likely to be forgiven for not completing long and complex tasks. For instance, if you use other prioritization methods and have a 3-hour task unfinished after a week, people will naturally wonder why you cannot complete a 3-hour task when you have an entire week. Not everything you do is relevant to them, so they may not care what else you need to do. Now they may build a perception that you can't even complete a simple task. On the other hand, if you have a 2-day task that is unfinished at the end of the week but have finished many small tasks, they will most likely feel that you have done your best and excuse you.

By refreshing the priority each time new tasks are assigned or reaffirmed, you minimize waste by reducing time spent on tasks that are no longer needed. You can quickly react to changes and return to task execution without spending time second guessing the importance and urgency of the tasks from the perspective of your company, team, manager and peers. Such priority setting is very straightforward because it is based on how fast you can perform the tasks and not on other criteria, which can be ambiguous or even contradictory, and these usually take time to evaluate. You will have more time on task execution rather than the administrative process of priority planning.

There is another benefit to use this method. In the last session when we discussed good time management habits, one of them is avoid multitasking. Multitasking is switching between tasks, which basically means that one task is interrupted by another. When you have less situational control over your work environment, you are more vulnerable to multitasking because you cannot say no to many requests coming your way. Chances of being interrupted are higher as you perform longer tasks, which will impact your overall task completion ability. By doing the shortest tasks first, you reduce the probability of further delays and increase your control over your plan. Overall, this method will boost your motivation and help to build a positive attitude.

Pros and Cons of Time-based Prioritization

- Advantages
    - Promote fast action
    - Complete more tasks in a given period
    - Build a reputation for being results oriented
    - Minimize waste by reducing time spent on tasks that are no longer needed
    - Lower the probability of interruption and multitasking, enabling better control

- Disadvantages
    - Blocked when not able to finish in estimated time
    - Postpone difficult tasks and snowball into a bigger problem

Slide 39

No one method is perfect in every situation, so there are a couple shortcomings in practicing this time-based prioritization method. The first issue is due to errors in estimating the task time or delays caused by unforeseen problems. After the task has been executing for a while, you find that it takes a lot of extra time to finish. You are now facing a difficult decision whether to stop or continue. If you use other prioritization methods, you don't need to decide and just keep going until it is done. If you stop, it seems that your time has been wasted. If you continue, you may be at risk of not completing any task. This situation creates stress and pressure that may affect your concentration and performance.

My recommendation for dealing with this situation is to inform the affected parties and ask them for suggestions. If they rely on you to complete this task, you need to continue to focus on it and request for help on this tasks or other tasks. Sometimes due to delay or scope changes, other options are used as backups, so this task is no longer needed and can be stopped. In any case, hopefully, you will take steps to prevent this from happening again. You need to ensure that the data used for estimation is accurate, which is no different from any other planning activity. If the task turns out to more complex than originally thought or you discover additional tasks that were not anticipated, it may be worth a discussion to still deliver value but maybe with a reduced scope so that the task can be completed with minimum additional time. When in doubt, ask experts and experienced colleagues.

The second issue is postponing difficult tasks to the end and having the possibility of snowballing into a bigger problem. The solution to this problem is to divide your work time into two periods. If a difficult task is deemed to be significantly important, then set aside a period of time each day to work on it. The rest of time will continue to use the time-based prioritization method. This combination seems to be a hybrid of time-based and priority matrix methods. That is right. You should split your work time into two parts and apply different methods to prioritize tasks.

There is another prioritization method that incorporate other factors and time to deal with the disadvantages mentioned. The Scaled Agile Framework (SAFe) in project management apples a method called Weighted Shortest Job First (WSJF) to prioritize jobs based on the economics of product development flow [8]. WSJF is a numerical factor that can be calculated by dividing the Cost of Delay (CoD) by the Job Duration [9]. The Cost of Delay is a combination of the weighted user-business value, time criticality and risk reduction-opportunity enablement value using the Fibonacci sequence (1, 2, 3, 5, 8, 13, 20, etc.) This method addresses some of the disadvantages of a pure time-based prioritization method, but you need to spend some time to set up a system to determine the user and business value, criticality, risk and opportunity enablement factors. This may not be easy when you are new to the organization, so you should start with the time-based method.

> How to design a task plan to achieve exceptional results?

I have mentioned several times that time-based prioritization works best when you have less situational control. At the beginning of your career, you spend most of your time working on the tasks assigned to you. Let's name this time as time for others (TFO). As your career progresses, you will be able to initiate tasks and gain more control over your work. At this point, you will need a separate time to perform tasks that you consider important. Let's name this time as time for yourself (TFY). Your TFY will increase as your career progresses, and how you use this time can significantly affect your career success. I am about to show you how to develop a task plan to achieve exceptional results beyond the expectations of your manager, clients or colleagues.

Developing a Task Plan for Exceptional Results

- Your work time can be divided into time for others (TFO) and time for yourself (TFY)
- Tasks can be separated by meeting and exceeding management expectation
    - Assigned tasks are below the expectation line and are done using TFO
    - Not all tasks below the line are assigned
    - Some tasks below the line are done using TFY
    - All tasks above the expectation line use TFY
    - Tasks above the line should be kept secret to produce surprising elements
- It is difficult to advance your career without TFY

Slide 40

You decide what to do in your TFY. Is it time to practice the priority matrix method based on the importance and urgency of the tasks? Not exactly. Ideally, you don't want to operate in a fire-fighting mode. In other words, you shouldn't wait until something becomes urgent before making it a priority. It is possible to perform urgent tasks occasionally, but in most cases, you should have more control in what you do at your own pace. Hence, prioritizing tasks based on urgency should be an exception rather than the norm. Under normal circumstances, you should plan tasks based on their impact. However, how do you determine the impact of the tasks?

Let's first discuss the notion of job expectation. When you are hired for a job, there is a set of responsibilities and duties that you are expected to perform. Employees who have just reached their job expectations are likely to be considered just successful, but if they want to be promoted, they need to perform additional responsibilities and extra duties. To help you advance your career, we should work together to identify activities that are below or above your management expectation, as shown on Slide #41.

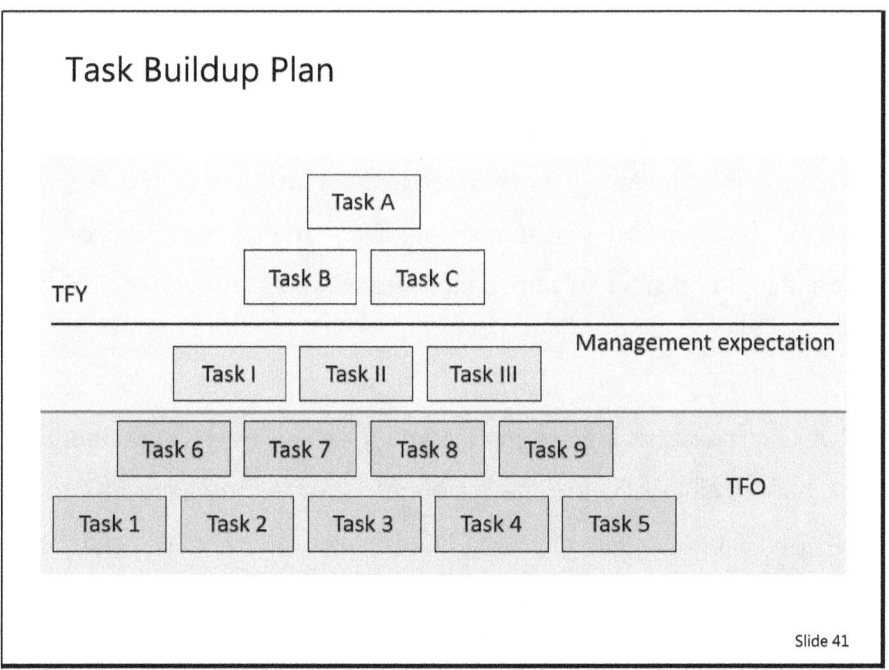

We start with the absolutely required tasks and build this task plan from bottom up. At the very bottom, we list the tasks that you must perform, or you may be fired. The next level will then consist of tasks with some flexibility, such as tasks that you initiate instead of being assigned. Continue building tasks until you have listed all the tasks that management expects you to perform. You can then draw a line on top. To go above and beyond the call of duty, you must continue to originate tasks above the line. By completing these tasks, you can surprise your management and pave the way for achieving exceptional results and career advancement.

This method can be applied to almost everything you do. Depending on the situation, management expectation can be replaced with client expectation, team expectation, etc. The important thing is to see what people expect of you and put extra effort to surprise them. In the case of finding a job, for example, we first determine what the hiring manager expects by studying the job description and the hiring company carefully and thoroughly. To increase the chance of being hired, you must identify things that exceed the expectation of the interviewers, then find ways to promote and maximize the effects of these things and strive to surprise the interviewers in order to deliver a good and long-lasting impression.

Obviously, tasks that are assigned to you are all below the expectation line, but not all tasks below the line are assigned. As you advance into senior positions, you are expected to take initiatives to resolve and prevent problems. Both TFO and TFY are used for the tasks below the expectation line. Tasks above the expectation line should be kept secret, so they are done using TFY only. If people are aware of these tasks, they will become expectations and no longer has the element of surprise. Therefore, if you do not have TFY, it is difficult to advance your career. You need to make time for TFY using the technique introduced in the previous session. Usually, it may also include using your personal time for TFY, which means working overtime.

How to initiate tasks and determine their impact?

Initiating Tasks and Determining Their Impact

- Seek tasks from two value propositions:
    - Eliminating waste – solving problems
    - Creating value – preventing problems
- Use a scoring system to assess the impact of tasks
    - Waste elimination tasks: the probability and severity of the problem
    - Value creation tasks: the opportunity and creativity of the proposal
- Effectively utilizing TFY means initiating and executing tasks based on the order of impact: solving the bigger problem or maximizing the return on time investment

Slide 42

When you have the freedom to initiate tasks, how do you find and determine which task to perform? You can start with two value propositions: waste elimination and value creation. Tasks in the waste elimination value proposition aim at reducing deficiencies in current systems, which often means identifying inefficiencies and resolving problems. Tasks in the value creation value proposition are proactively changing current systems to increase benefits or prevent undesired issues from reoccurring.

In order to clearly understand the difference in the two value propositions, we can take the operation of the fire department as an example. The waste elimination tasks are improvements to the firefighting operation, which may include shortening response processes, keeping equipment reliable and improving the skills and fitness of the personnel, whereas the value creation tasks are preventive in nature, such as community outreach programs, which may include educating the public on fire prevention and performing targeted inspections of old buildings.

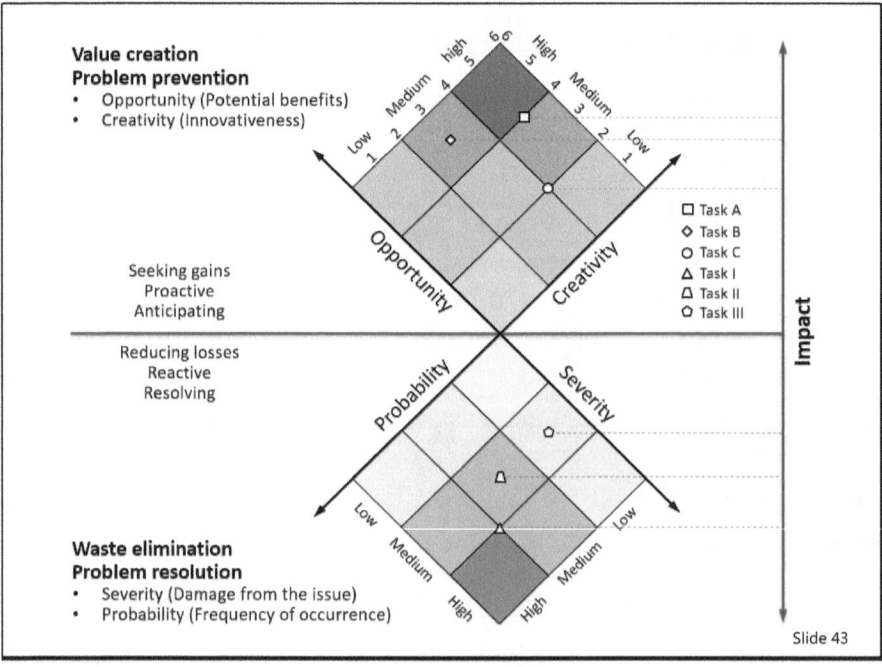

To use TFY effectively, you need to initiate enough tasks to completely fill it. The order of execution should be based on the impact of the tasks. For tasks in the waste elimination value proposition, the order of impact is based on a combined rating of the probability and severity of the problem, which essentially means solving the biggest issue first. For tasks in the value creation value proposition, the order of impact is maximizing gains based on a combined rating of the potential benefits and innovativeness of the proposal. Slide #43 illustrates the task impact profiling of the example tasks shown on Slide #41. Task A, B and C are tasks above the expectation line, whereas Task I, II and III are tasks below the line.

Example Task Impact Order Worksheet

Task	Waste Elimination			Value Creation			Total Score	Impact Order
	Probability	Severity	Score	Opportunity	Creativity	Score		
Task A			0.00	4	5	6.36	6.36	1
Task B			0.00	5	3	5.66	5.66	3
Task C			0.00	2	4	4.24	4.24	5
Task I	4	4	5.66			0.00	5.69	2
Task II	3	3	4.24			0.00	4.26	4
Task III	1	3	2.83			0.00	2.84	6

Scale: 0-6 with 6 the highest

Score(WE)=Probability*Sin(45°)+Severity*Cos(45°)
Score(VC)=Opportunity*Sin(45°)+Creativity*Cos(45°)
Total Score= Score(WE)*1.005+Score(VC)

Slide 44

As an alternative to mapping tasks graphically as shown on Slide #43, a simple Excel worksheet can be created using formulas to calculate the impact of tasks. The table on Slide #44 illustrates the rating assessments of the same tasks shown on Slide #43. The score for a waste elimination task is calculated by "=Probability*Sin(45°)+Severity*Cos(45°)" and for a value creation task, it is "=Opportunity*Sin(45°)+Creativity*Cos(45°)."

Should two tasks arrive at the same score, a clear order can be achieved by modifying the ratings or adding a weighted factor in the total score formula. When two tasks score the same and belong to the same category, we can reassess either or both ratings. When two tasks have the same score but belong to different categories, we can assign a higher weight to one category. In the example, we consider that tasks in waste elimination have a greater impact than those in value creation. The total score formula is thus "=Score(WE)*1.005+Score(VC)," where Score(WE) is the score of the waste elimination task, and Score(VC) is the score of the value creation task on the same row. The number 1.005 is the multiplier I chose to use in this case. If you have an Excel template setup, it will be fairly quick to assess a task at the time of initiation to determine where to put it in your schedule.

You now have a completed picture of task prioritization. For assigned tasks using TFO, you should use the time-based prioritization method and perform the shortest task first. For self-initiating tasks using TFY, you should execute them in the order of impact. In other words, when doing things for others, focus on the turnaround time and getting things done quickly. When doing things for yourself, focus on obtaining the best gains or avoiding the worst damages.

This follows simple logic. When you are doing things for other, you play a support role, so you should trust the task assigners on the necessity of the tasks. You don't need to second guess the importance of the tasks, just execute one by one to remove them from your calendar as quickly as possible. The same logic does not apply to doing tasks for yourself. For instance, getting a graduate degree takes a long time, and you will not get to it if you use time-based prioritization. Therefore, you need to do your tasks based on benefits rather than time. Once you have determined that a task is important to you, make time to do it even if you don't have the time.

> What is risk management?

Thus far, we have established general guidelines for initiating and prioritizing tasks. Since we are not living in a perfect world, in some special cases the guidelines will not work perfectly. There is uncertainty in what we do, which brings risks. Addressing task risks is indispensable part of task management.

Traditional Risk Management

- Focus on risk containment
  - The process: risk identification, risk analysis, risk planning, and risk monitoring and control
  - The objective: lower the risk probability, reduce the impact severity or both
- Risk identification methods are brainstorming, using past analogies, soliciting expert opinions, assessing cause-effect relations, and ranking the accuracy of data and assumptions
- Risk mitigation tactics are risk transfer, risk reduction, risk avoidance and contingency planning

Slide 45

Traditionally, risk management is defined as the identification and evaluation of risks followed by mitigations to avoid or minimize the impact of unfortunate events. This is reflected in Traditional Project

Management where risk management generally comprises the process of risk identification, risk analysis, risk planning and risk monitoring and control. Risk identification is a process of identifying all potential risks associated with a project or a task. Risk identification methods include brainstorming, using past analogies, soliciting expert opinions, assessing cause-effect relations, and ranking the accuracy of data and assumptions.

Risk analysis is to classify risks into different categories from high to low using Risk Profile or Risk Matrix. A typical Risk Profile is shown on Slide #46. Risks are analyzed based on the probability of occurrence and the severity of impact. For instance, high risk items have a high probability and high severity. Additional planning, monitoring and controlling efforts should be devoted to high risk items.

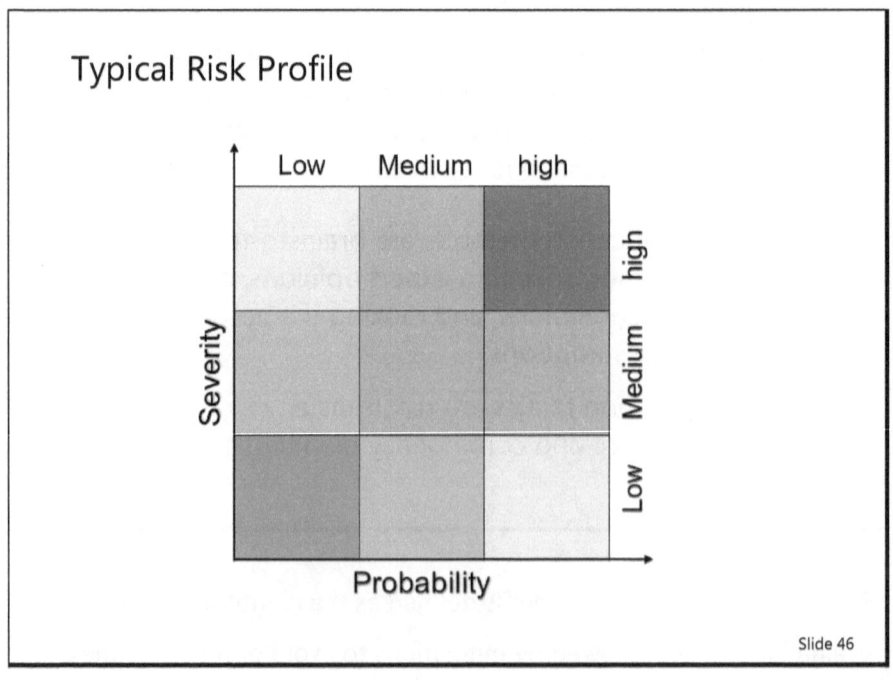

Risk planning is defining the mitigation tactics that can lower the risk probability, reduce the impact severity or both. Such tactics are risk transfer, risk reduction, risk avoidance and contingency planning. Risk transfer is giving the risk to someone else, such as asking an experienced colleague or the client to do the risky part of a task. Risk reduction is using the best way to do a task, such as buying the best tools or materials. Risk avoidance is eliminating risky activities by minimizing complexity or reducing scope of the deliverable. Contingency planning is having backups, buffers or insurance.

Risk monitoring and control means collecting status information and taking actions to implement the mitigation tactics while tasks are being executed. Monitoring is not limited to finding the current state but also the progressing trends. Actions taken in risk control can be corrective or preventive. What I have just described is the overall scope of risk management in project management, which is only risk containment.

Effective risk management mean more than containing risks. Certain tasks will bring significant benefits but also accompany with substantial uncertainties. If you want to realize these benefits, risk-taking is often necessary, which means pushing yourself to the limit. We are living in a competitive world. If you are unwilling to take risks, you will most likely lose the opportunity to others who are willing to do so. Hence, playing it safe and not taking a risk is a potential risk in of itself. However, you also need to know your limits as taking risks foolishly will also do more harm than good. Therefore, comprehensive risk management should include both risk containment and risk-taking.

> ## Comprehensive Risk Management
>
> - Comprehensive risk management should include risk-taking in addition to risk containment
> - Risk containment is for tasks below the expectation line
>   - Analyze risk based on probability and severity
>   - Take actions to avoid and minimize risks
> - Risk-taking is for tasks above the expectation line
>   - Analyze risk based on creativity and opportunity
>   - Take actions to create and maximize surprises
>   - Keep the above the line activities confidential to create a psychologically safe environment for you to take risks
>
> Slide 47

> When to contain risks and when to take risks? And how?

Whether to use risk containment or risk-taking depends on the nature of the task. By modifying the task plan on Slide #41, what risk management measure to use is shown on Slide #48. In short, risk containment applies to tasks below the expectation line, and risk-taking applies to tasks above the line.

As described previously, tasks below the expectation line are either assigned to you or anticipated by you as expected by your manager, client or colleagues. They count on you to complete these tasks without surprise. Therefore, traditional risk management tactics still apply to containing the risk of these tasks, which means avoiding or minimizing risks so that tasks can be completed as expected.

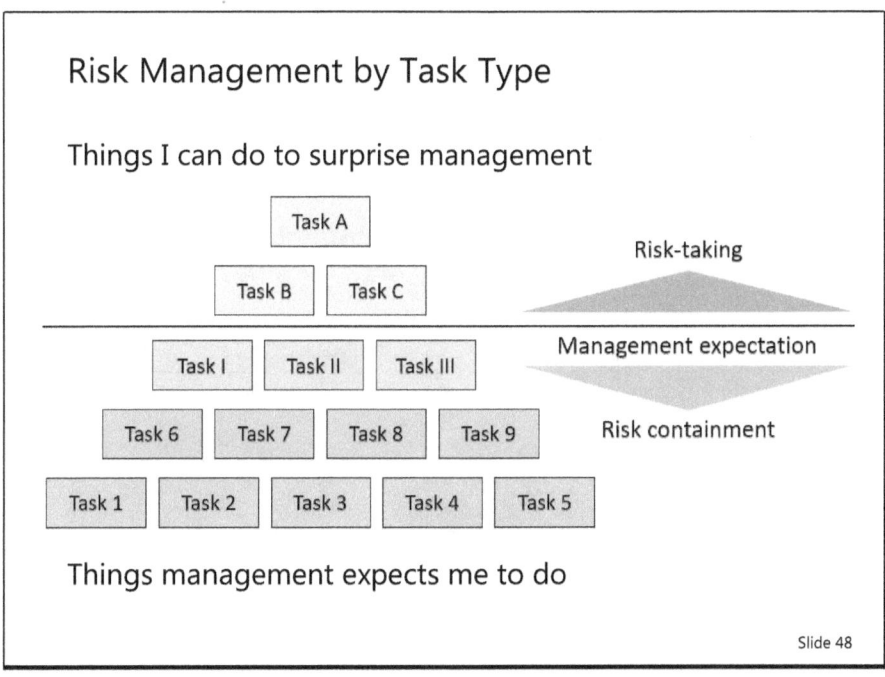

For tasks that are above the line, risk-taking should be highly encouraged. What does risk-taking mean? It generally means maximizing creativity and creating opportunity, which constitutes the profile for risk-taking. As shown on Slide #49, this risk-taking profile has been added to the traditional risk containment profile (shown on Slide #46) to form a comprehensive risk management profile. The added profile is the mirror image of the traditional profile, separated by the management expectation line, but with different axis labels. This illustration looks almost the same as the task impact profile shown on Slide #43. However, risks are mapped in the profile instead of tasks. The "Impact" axis is replaced by "Degree of Surprise."

"Degree of Surprise" is used for the vertical axis instead of "Degree of Expectation" because "expectation" only applies to tasks below the expectation line. Tasks above the line are thus not expected by management so "surprise" is a better term. The two terms are inversely correlated as a higher degree of expectation means a lower degree of surprise. Along the vertical Degree of Surprise axis, risk level decreases from the bottom to the up while the motivation of risk-taking increases. This means you should take more conservative approaches when executing lower tasks on the risk profile.

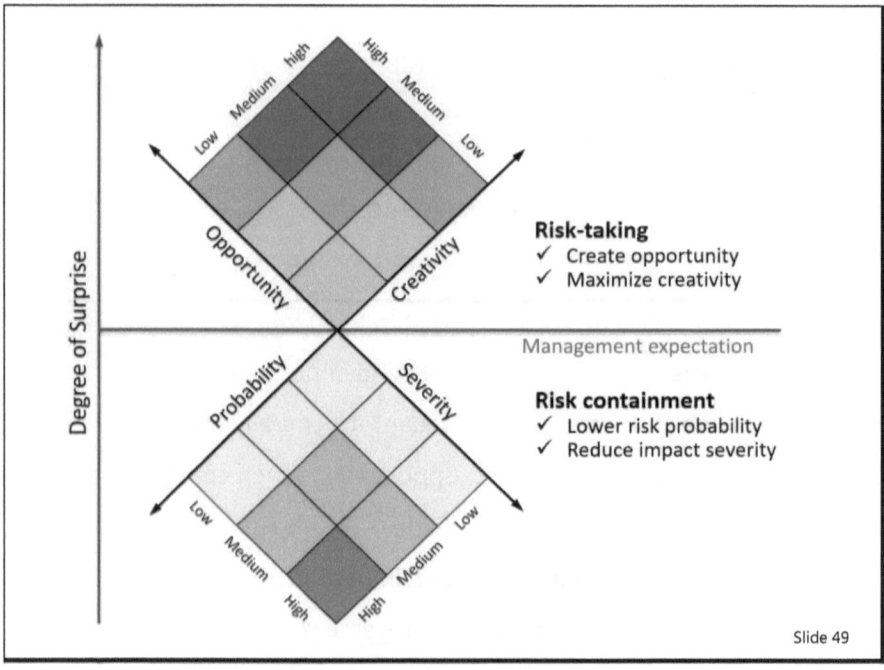

When analyzing risk with this profile, in addition to the traditional high, medium and low risk levels determined by probability and severity ratings, you now also have the high, medium and low surprise levels determined by creativity and opportunity ratings. You can use acronyms to represent these levels, such as HR (high risk), MR (medium risk), LR (low risk), LS (low surprise), MS (medium surprise) and HS (high surprise).

Creativity is along the same axis of probability. Reducing the probability of risk typically involves taking a more conservative approach to reducing the chance of failure. As reliability theory indicates, the reliability of a system is the multiplication of the reliabilities of all its components. As such, a simpler system is more reliable since the probability of failure is lower, because there are fewer components. Maximizing creativity generally means generating new features and functions, which will naturally increase the probability of failure. You need to keep these features and functions secret from management, so the penalty of failure is much lower. This provides a psychologically safe environment for you to take risks; even if some of them fail, there would be no impact to you as management is not aware that these features and functions exist. On the other hand, if they are implemented successfully, you will attract greater attention from management and potentially bring greater surprises.

Along the same axis as severity and above the expectation line is where you will find the opportunities to provide management with surprising features. You should demonstrate how these new features could be beneficial. If your manager does not know how to use the new features, he or she will not know what to expect. These features will therefore have no connection to management expectation and thus developing them would be a waste of time and effort. It is fine to generate more features in the early stages of development with the understanding that not all of them will be successful. Following the "fail fast, fail forward" mentality, test and modify existing features and add new ones when you have time. More focus and effort should be given to features that have a high surprise rating.

What is the process flow for task management?

Now that you have a basic understanding of task prioritization, impact planning and risk management, we can step through the entire process of task management. The first step is to have a list of assigned tasks and update it as tasks come to you.

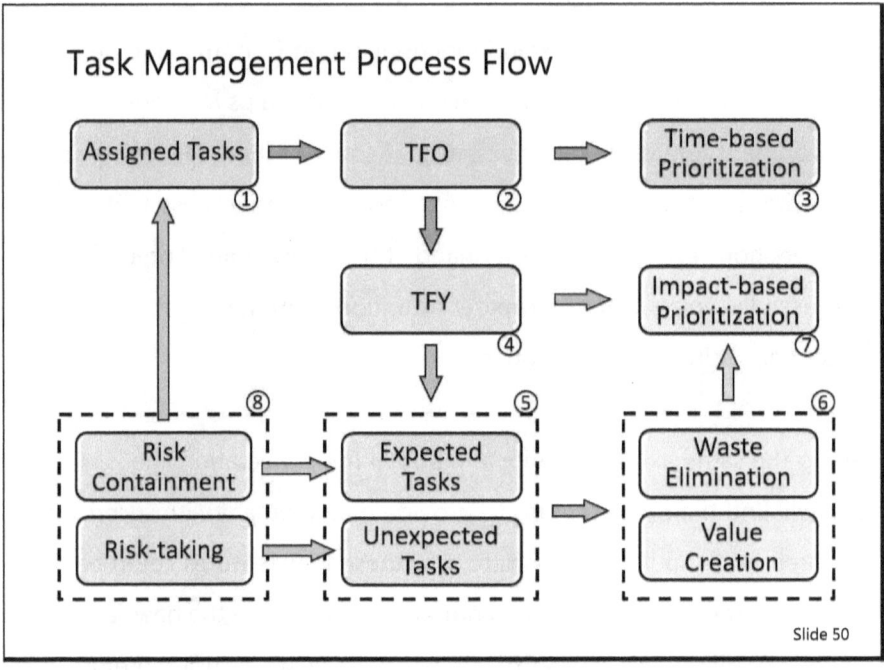

Second, roughly estimate the time needed for the assigned tasks and block out the TFO portion of your work time. You can do this weekly, bi-weekly or daily depending on the number of tasks and how often they are assigned. For ease of management, it is best to have a relatively stable TFO, but as new tasks are assigned, you may need to modify it. Third, use time-based prioritization method to prioritize assigned tasks, and start to execute the shortest task first, then the next shortest task, and so on.

Fourth, understand your TFY, which is your total work time minus TFO. At the beginning of your career, your TFO is usually larger than TFY. You need TFY to advance your career. The more TFY you have, the better you have control over your job. Therefore, you goal is to gradually reduce TFO and increase TFY over time. If you want to grow your career quickly, you often need to use your personal time for TFY.

Fifth, initiate tasks to fill your TFY. Start by listing tasks that management expects you to perform. You may confirm that these tasks are in fact expected tasks by anticipating whether management will be surprised when these tasks are done. Just performing the expected tasks will not take you to the next career level. Hence, you need to continue generating tasks that can surprise management. To keep these tasks unexpected by management, you need to execute them in secret to maximize the wow factor. It is fine to generate more tasks than your TFY allows, because we will prioritize them next.

Sixth, assess the impact of self-initiated tasks. To do this, we divide the tasks into two groups: waste elimination and value creation. Waste elimination is to solve existing problems that cause the inefficiency in the current system. The impact of a waste elimination task is a comprehensive assessment of the probability and severity of the issue. Value creation is developing new features that will bring new benefits and prevent future problems. The impact of a value creation task is the combined rating of its creativity and the opportunity it creates.

Seventh, rank the tasks according to their impact and execute them in order, solving the biggest problem first and going for the biggest gain.

Eighth, evaluate the risk of the tasks. For assigned and expected tasks, the risk containment strategy should be used. Identify the key risks for each task, and then analyze each risk based on its occurring frequency and potential damage. Pay more attention to planning, monitoring and controlling high risks, i.e. use multiple mitigation tactics. For unexpected tasks (in the viewpoint of management), the risk-taking strategy applies. Identify the key features that each task will bring, then evaluate each feature based on its creativity and potential opportunities. Dedicate more effort to the high surprise features to maximize your return on investment. By the way, completing all features or unexpected tasks should not be your goal. Completing one or two unexpected tasks should be enough to surprise people. So just do it. If it fails, it's okay because your management doesn't know it. It does take your time and energy, but this will not be a complete loss since you gain knowledge to perform better in the future. In fact, you should not do too much in one round, because the more you do, the more people expect of you. You may set an expectation that you cannot continue to meet.

The eight-step process described here is a general guideline to task management. There are other factors that can affect the use of this process. First and foremost, your success in task management depends on your time management practices. If you do not have good time management habits and the ability to make time, it is difficult to pursue all tasks, especially tasks that are beyond expectation of others. That is why we discuss time management before task management. Good time management can cope with some inefficiencies in task management. For instance, you may not need to prioritize assigned tasks if you can make time to do them all within the required time. Task prioritization depends heavily on how much time you have. The amount of TFY determines your ability to achieve exceptional results beyond people's expectations.

Session 4 Summary: Managing Your Tasks

- Apply different tactics for the 3 types of tasks

	Task Type		
	Assigned	Expected	Unexpected
Main objective	Quick action	Resolution	Prevention
Time category	TFO	TFY	TFY
Prioritization	Completion time	Probability & severity	Opportunity & creativity
Rick management	Containment	Containment	Risk-taking

- Use the task management process as a guide while making adjustments as circumstances warrant
- Task management, time management and situation management are interrelated and impact each other

Slide 51

The application of task management practices is also situational. We set the general direction and did not go into special cases. In some cases, problem prevention is expected, or problem resolution is unexpected because the problem is very large. Special cases also apply to assigned tasks. As we discussed earlier, individuals often do not have much situational control early in their careers because tasks are usually assigned. You may be in a situation where your manager is very authoritarian and controlled. As a result, you have no choice but to prioritize all tasks assigned by this manager over other project managers and teams.

Clearly, your ability to control your work environment affects the way you manage tasks. The worst case is that you have to do exactly what others tell you, including what and when. If you are your own boss, there will be no assigned tasks. You may still need to perform some expected tasks for customers and subordinates. The best case is having total control where no one expects you to do anything. You cannot classify tasks as expected tasks and unexpected tasks, at which point, you choose your own path to define and execute tasks. Improved situational control enhances your ability to manage tasks. Managing your environment is the subject of the next section, and we will discuss how to improve situational control.

Session 4 Exercise – Plan your tasks

Step 1. Analyze assigned tasks

List assigned tasks & estimate completion time:
(Recommended weekly but may be daily if you have frequent assigned tasks. Skip if no assigned task.)

Tasks by Week	Time Needed
	hours
	hours
	hours
	hours
	hours
	hours
	hours
	hours
	hours
	hours
Total TFO Needed	hours

Step 2&3. Set TFO, select and prioritize assigned tasks within TFO

Total allocated TFO: _____ hours/week; _____ hours/day

Order	To-do Tasks	Day
1		Mon.
2		Mon.- Tue.
3		
4		
5		
6		
7		

Step 4. Determine your TFY

> Your total work time: _____ hours/week; _____ hours/day
>
> Your TFO: _____ hours/week; _____ hours/day
>
> Calculate total work time – TFO and get
>
> Available Work TFY: _____ hours/week; _____ hours/day
>
> Go back to Session 3 Exercise #1 Step 2, copy the hours left per week: _____ hours, add to Work TFY and get
>
> Total available TFY: _____ hours/week; _____ hours/day

Step 5&6. Generate tasks for your TFY and assess their impact

> **List expected tasks & brainstorm unexpected tasks:**
> (Recommended using the Excel template on Slide #44 to assess impact. May enter the score or order in the last column.)
>
> | **Expected Tasks** | **Time Needed** | **Impact** |
> |---|---|---|
> | | hours | |
> | | hours | |
> | | hours | |
> | | hours | |
> | | hours | |
> | | hours | |
> | | hours | |
> | | hours | |
> | | hours | |
> | | hours | |
> | **Unexpected Tasks** | **Time Needed** | **Impact** |
> | | hours | |
> | | hours | |
> | | hours | |

Step 7. Set TFY, select and prioritize assigned tasks within TFY

Total allocated TFY: _____ hours/week; _____ hours/day

Order	To-do Tasks	Day
1		Mon.
2		Mon.- Tue.
3		
4		
5		
6		
7		

Step 8a. Risk containment plan

Identify risks of expected tasks: (Assessment & mitigation)

Risks	Rating	Planned Mitigation

Monitor high and medium risks. Review this plan regularly and take mitigation actions as planned.

Step 8b. Risk-taking wish list

List the possible features of unexpected tasks: (Value assessment & surprise rating)

Features	Rating	Potential Benefits

Focus on the high surprise features. The goal is completing 1 to 2 items per round. It is okay to drop or push items to a punch list for the next round.

Session 5

Managing Your Environment

Obtain situational control

Session 5: Managing Your Environment

"You are a product of your environment." - W. Clement Stone

Be aware of your environment and influence it.

Managing relations
- Build and influence your close circles

Managing communication
- "Communication - the human connection - is the key to personal and career success." - Paul J. Meyer

Managing situations
- "Control your situation don't let your situations to control you..." - Debi Saha

Slide 53

What are the main components of a good work environment?

When you decide to accept a job offer, you are actually choosing your work environment, which is an important determinant. In fact, many people prefer a good working environment over salary. A good work environment usually means having good people, collaboration, corporate policies and physical environment. In most cases, corporate policies and physical environment are beyond your control. Your ability to change them is very low, so what you usually can do is research and avoid companies that have intolerable policies and environments. In this session, we will focus on the areas that you can control, starting with how to build and manage relations through networking and influencing. Next, we discuss effective communication techniques that enhance collaboration. Finally, we will go over some general guidelines for dealing with difficult situations.

Good Work Environment

- Corporate values, policies and physical environment
    - Research and avoid companies that you cannot tolerate
    - Pay a visit and go with your feeling
- People
    - Build your professional network
    - Apply influence tactics for career advancement
- Collaboration
    - Improve emotional intelligence to discover the hidden needs and messages of others
    - Effectively communicate your ideas

Slide 54

Although you do not have much control over company policies and physical environment, you certainly have choices for selecting a company that best fits your work style. Therefore, I want to briefly discuss how to see through the visual artifacts of a company and look into your own personality to determine if the company is right for you.

How to determine if a company suits your personality and work style?

We have different working styles, which are derived from our personality. There are also a variety of work environments across companies, which depend on the corporate cultures and industry requirements. For instance, some companies value creativity, while others demand discipline. You will be more comfortable working in an environment that suits your personality. Corporation generally implement policies to ensure that the desired working environment is maintained. Therefore, by researching the policies of a company, you can determine whether this company provides a good working environment for you. If you cannot tolerate certain company policies, your success will be limited.

Another way to determine if a company's work environment is right for you is to pay a visit. A company's physical environment conveys powerful messages of the corporation's operating philosophy and culture. For instance, a workplace filled of art decorations indicates the company values creativity, and a clean and organized workplace generally promotes discipline.

Based on a study done by the Aberdeen Group, about 61% of new employees made the decision whether to stay at the company within the first month of employment and about 26% new employees made the decision within the first week [10]. A month is typically not enough time for employees to have a full understanding of the corporate policies and culture. That typically takes 6-12 months, so these employees made decisions based on their impressions of the artifacts. Often, if you ask these people what factors into the decision to leave, they either cannot describe their reasons clearly or pick on some minor and superficial details. In large part, they developed the feeling that the company is not suitable for them. The result is a lack of commitment to the company, and they are just waiting for the next opportunity to leave. Therefore, you should pay attention to how you feel in a particular workplace, as your emotions depend on your personality and values. Trust your basic intuition, if you feel uncomfortable, this company may not be right for you.

What are the key elements in managing professional relations?

The most important element in the work environment is people. The company is founded and established by people, with its policies, culture and physical environment. People skills are extremely critical for career success. First, you need to build your own professional network, then maintain your network through regular engagements, and finally, apply influence tactics for mutual gains.

Managing Professional Relations

- Intentional networking
    - Identify key networking targets
    - Seek networking opportunities
    - Maintain professional relationships with the right interface frequency and genuine reasons
    - Improve your ability to help others

- Influence with sensitivity and flexibility
    - Master and practice different styles situationally: push, pull and disengage
    - Manage various working relationships: up, across, and down

Slide 55

There is no doubt that developing a professional network is essential for career development. Professional networking is intentionally developing professional relationships to share information and resources for mutual gains. Networking is not a discrete activity that you do only when you need something. It is a lifestyle that requires regular engagement. However, this does not mean going to all networking events and spending time with everyone you know. You need to invest time wisely and effectively. Therefore, you should conduct selective networking by first identifying key targets.

How to prioritize your networking effort?

Sales professionals use a color dot exercise shown on Slide #56 to identify and reach the key decision makers. We can use the same exercise to identify networking targets who can help you advance your career. This exercise uses black, green and blue color dots to create a networking map with people around you.

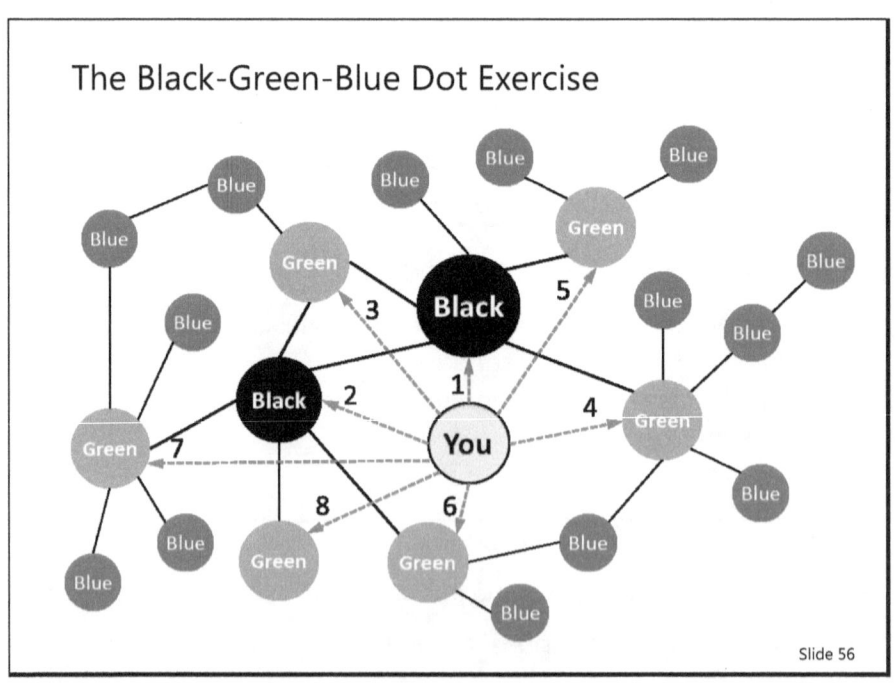

Black dots are people who have the power to make decisions that can affect your career, such as managers of departments in which you want to work in the future. Green dots are people who the black dots trust and often consult for decision-making. They can be the right-hand person to the manager or the senior technical lead in the group. Blue dots, also referred to as "Smurfs" by salespeople in this exercise, are people who have minimal effect on your career.

You can start the exercise by listing the people around you. If you are working and networking within your company, it is easier to start with the organizational chart and then color the individuals on the chart. Identify the black dots first. There may be multiple black dots who have different levels of impact on you, so you can use larger and smaller dots to represent them. As indicated on Slide #56, the example shows two black dots. Networking with the larger black dot is the number one priority and the smaller black dot is number two. If you are networking for future opportunities, pick a few organizations where you want to get a job and start to map out the people. In many cases, you may not know the black dots or even their names. You should seek information from your existing network and social media, such as LinkedIn.

It is typical that you do not have frequent interactions with the black dots, especially if you have ambitious goals. That is why networking with the green dots is important. You need to prioritize your time and effort on green dots who are resourceful and have connections with multiple black dots. Next are the green dots who are more active and given greater responsibility. A networking priority order from 1 to 8 is shown on Slide #56. You should take time to thoroughly review the networking map and understand the reasons behind the order.

How about blue dots? Blue dots are sources of information for you to map and connect to the green and black dots. If you are new to the environment and have not yet established connections with the green and black dots, you need to start networking with the blue dots, but maintain a professional level relationship. Getting too close and personal quickly may cause problems and undesirable situations in the future. Blue dots who are aggressive in their career advancement will likely be your competitors. Blue dots who are happy with where they are usually demand more of your time, which you may not have much when you are actively pursuing higher career goals in the future. We will discuss this in detail shortly in the managing peer relationships section.

Obviously, you should see yourself at the same level as the blue dots. Your networking priority targets, the black and green dots, should be the people who are more successful than you in at least one aspect of the field you are pursuing. As you advance your career to become a peer of the green dots, you should update your networking map and identify new green and black dots. You may have one networking map with people in your company and another one covering the industry. Also, as you explore different career paths in different companies, you may have multiple networking maps.

How to seek networking opportunities inside your company?

Once you have identified your networking targets, you need to look for opportunities to connect with them. The approach is simple, going where your targets may appear. As Woody Allen put it, "Eighty percent of success is showing up." Slide #57 lists some opportunities that you should be aware of, but there are many others. When your networking targets are inside your company, you should pay attention to meetings and events that involve your targets' business unit, such as regular business update meetings and open forums. As you attend these meetings, ask questions when you have the opportunity and stay at the end of the meeting to introduce yourself to your target.

Seeking Networking Opportunities

- Networking inside your company
    - Business update meetings and open forums
    - Volunteering and community support events
    - Employee groups and hobby activities
- Networking outward
    - Professional seminars, conferences, symposiums and online forums
    - Industry associations and business clubs
    - University classes, open talks and alumni events
    - Volunteering for nonprofit organizations and community groups
    - Social media, trade shows, career and job fairs

Slide 57

In most companies, especially large ones, many activities do not have clear ownership, and some activities are supported by volunteers intentionally. For example, emergency incidents will originate many unplanned tasks that require additional resources, such as the recent COVID-19 pandemic. By stepping up to provide voluntary support for the coordination of some business contingency efforts, I have established connections with senior executives in the Emergency Operations Center (EOC). In distress situations, your efforts will be more appreciated, so you stand out from your peers. However, you must have time in these situations while others are busy dealing with their own responses to the distress situation. This is another reason why the ability to make time is critical.

Of course, emergencies do not happen often, and you should not rely on these situations to volunteer. There are many normal activities that require voluntary support. I began volunteering for company events, emergency response teams, as well as progressively supporting employee training facilitation, career advising and new employee orientation. Another example is my voluntary support for translations in hosting delegates from countries and regions that speak my native language, which has given me many opportunities to work closely with senior executives and the CEO of the company. I believe there are more opportunities than you think, you just need to look for them. Again, you must practice time management to make time available, so that you are prepared to seize the opportunity when it comes.

In addition, many companies promote corporate social responsibilities by encouraging employees to volunteer in education and community involvement events. Senior executives and managers should be role modeling participation, so joining these events gives you the opportunity to interact with them. Therefore, you should pay attention to your company's volunteer service activities, or even better organize an event and approach your networking targets for support. This creates direct interactions with the people you want to network, and it is difficult to reject you if you find a volunteer service with a good cause. Joining employee groups also provide opportunities for networking. Many companies form employee groups to support diversity demonstrating that the company is a great place to work for all employees. For example, my company provides annual funding to support various employee groups. Some are based on ethnicity, such as Asian, Hispanic, African American, etc. Some are religion, related such as Christianity, Islam, Hinduism, etc. There are also groups for women, new college graduates and doctorate professionals. Many of these groups have senior leaders as sponsors and organize events with other senior leaders invited.

In addition to the formal employee groups supported by the company, there are other groups that are formed by employees enjoying certain activities, such as sports teams, hiking groups, and hobby groups. Of course, you need to find out what activities your networking targets enjoy. For example, if you find your target enjoys playing golf, you can arrange a tournament and ask that individual to participate or support the event. You can also pay attention to the routine of your networking targets. For instance, an executive at our company regularly exercise in the company gym. Following the same routine and showing up in the gym during this time increases your chance of building a relationship with this executive. There are many opportunities that you could spend time and energy actively seeking.

How to find external networking opportunities?

When networking externally, there are many venues you can connect with professionals in your area of interest. You can start by attending seminars, workshops, conferences and symposiums related to your field. There are also open houses and company tours available locally. Joining targeted online forums and chat groups allows you to access the information on these events. You can also find wide range of events online from sites like Meetup and Eventbrite. Since many of these events are organized by industry associations and business clubs, joining these organizations allows you to connect directly with the professionals in your area. You can participate in events that are only available to their members and build deeper relationships with other members.

Academia is another channel for networking. If you can commit to a degree program, you can build good relationships with classmates and professors while improving your skills. For instance, one of the key selling points of the EMBA program is the access to a network of executives. Even if you are not pursuing a degree program, taking open university courses at certain universities can also provide similar opportunities. If you live in the San Francisco bay Area, you can take courses offered by Stanford Continuing Studies or UC Berkeley Extension, attended by many working professionals. If you live elsewhere, there should be local universities for working professionals to improve their skills. In addition to regular courses, many universities offer free lectures and open talks throughout the academic years. I do not recommend taking online courses, since they do not provide a good networking opportunity. Traditional classroom courses give you face-to-face interaction, which is an important part of building relationships. Online courses do offer convenience and are useful for learning certain skills. We will cover the learning aspect in the next session. Finally, joining your school's alumni association and participating in its events also gives you the opportunity to connect with successful alumni.

We have already mentioned that volunteering is an important way to create networking opportunities inside the company. It can also be used for external networking. If you have time, consider volunteering for nonprofit organizations and community groups. Many non-profit organizations have corporate executives on their boards. Not only can you support a cause you care about, you can also connect with other professionals who are willing and enthusiastic about helping others. Community groups are less formal than the nonprofit organizations and typically support local causes. Examples of community groups are religious and church groups, youth mentoring and sports leagues, fire department support and emergency preparedness corps, police support and neighborhood watch. It is easier to develop close relationships when participating in these community services.

Other external networking opportunities include online networking using social media, trade shows as well as career and job fairs, but these are less effective and require a lot of follow-up efforts. Social media is very popular, especially among the younger generations. However, it is very difficult to establish in-depth professional relationships through online interactions alone. Meeting the other party face-to-face demonstrates that you are interested and willing to take time for personal engagement. In-person conversations allow both parties to express feelings more clearly and in a more personal way. Using social media to connect but creating opportunities for in-person interactions is still necessary.

Trade shows and exhibitions usually attract large crowds. However, since their main purpose is to promote business, in-depth information exchange and personal interaction are difficult. You may receive many business cards from event participants but building a relationship with any of them requires additional follow-up. Even when you follow up, don't be surprised if they cannot recall who you are, because they met so many people at the event. Likewise, attending career and job fairs allows you to interface directly with a few employees in companies you are interested in, but building relationships with these employees is also difficult. Unless you really stand out you are competing with all the other attendees for their attention.

There are other networking opportunities based on hobbies, politics, religion and lifestyle. You should prioritize your time for networking opportunities that yield optimal results. That means engaging in activities and participating in events that reflect the common interests of you and your networking targets.

> How to maintain professional relationships?

The networking opportunities we just discussed can only establish connections between you and your networking targets. Connection is just the beginning of relationship development. Just like any other relationship, professional relationships need to be cultivated and maintained. It is obvious that you must do a follow up shortly after the first meeting, and then how often you reach out requires careful consideration.

Form your own perspective, you need to balance the time spent on networking and other career development activities. If you believe maintaining professional relationships is full of all lunch socials and after-work drinks, you are on the wrong path. You do not need and should not spend a lot of time doing this. When it comes to meaningful relationships, quality trumps quantity. Occasional in-depth conversations are sufficient to sustain a professional relationship. You also need to look at this from your target's perspective. Because your primary focus is networking up, you should concentrate on networking with black dots and green dots. These people are more successful and usually busier than you. Constantly bugging them can lead to the opposite result, and they may avoid you to conserve their valuable time. However, not enough interfaces, you risk losing the relationships.

Maintaining Professional Relationships

- Follow up shortly after the first meeting
- Determine the frequency of interface
    - Balance your time, focusing on quality over quantity
    - Value the other party's time and don't overdo it
    - Prompt the next meeting time in each meeting
- Find genuine reasons for interface
    - Share information
    - Seek advice and ask for mentoring and coaching
- Enhance your capabilities and improve you position to provide value to the other party

Slide 58

So, what is a good frequency for the interfaces? Many people schedule the interface quarterly, monthly or on major holidays. It is easier to do, but I do not recommend this approach as it seems too mechanistic and lacks sincerity and personal touch. The interface frequency depends on the situation and the individual. For example, there are more opportunities for meeting with internal networking contacts. The best way is to prompt the next possible interface time each time you meet with the individual. You can do this by sharing your recent activities and projects and the expected completion time. In exchange, you draw the same information from the other party. After the other party shares the end date of his or her project, you can show an interest in knowing the results and suggest a meeting time when both parties are less busy. Do not push the other party to commit to an exact date and time for the next meeting. You can check with the individual to confirm the meeting when the time approaches.

You need to find genuine reasons to create interaction opportunities with your networking targets. Sharing information is one of the most common approaches, but the shared information should not be some random news that you find interesting. You must pay attention to the interests and activities of your networking targets and the shared information must be linked to these interests and activities. In addition to just sharing the information, you should also include comments, opinions or personal reflections. This demonstrates that you are genuinely interested in what the other party is doing and willing to take the time to have an in-depth discussion on the topic. You may also share your personal stories and future plans if you find a similar past or life path between you and the other party, which will build trust in the other party to form a strong relationship.

Seeking advice is another common way to reach out to your networking targets. You can purposely ask for help on a particular endeavor or formally request the individual to be your career mentor. If the individual agrees to be your mentor, you have a legitimate reason to hold regular meetings to discuss your career actions and plans.

I want to specifically point out that the best way to maintain a professional relationship is having the ability to help the other party. A healthy relationship must have mutual benefits for both parties. An imbalance in the relationship will not be long-lasting as only a few people can keep giving without receiving. Therefore, before you approach someone asking for favors, you need to think about what you can do to repay the support you receive. This does not mean that you can only have good relationships with people at your current career level. Do not assume that you have nothing to offer when you are networking with senior professionals. You can offer to take on administrative and logistic tasks to support activities involving the senior professional. Save them time in exchange for their guidance.

Your relationship with a senior professional can also be based on exchanging his or her current support with your future potential, much like making an investment for future benefits. As such, you must demonstrate hard work and build a reputation of having the potential for future success. Aggressively pursuing new skills and proactively sharing your progress with the senior professional will enhance this perception and maintain a supportive relationship. As a career advisor, I would love to see my efforts help my advisees become successful executives in the future. The more you invest in your career; the more people will invest in you. That is why it is important to continuously improve your capabilities, and we will discuss the topic of continuous learning in the next session.

> What are the influence tactics?

Whether you are building a professional network or working with your colleagues, you need to master the art of influence to maximize your effectiveness. In the early 1990s, I attended the *Positive Power and Influence* training program offered by the Situation Management Systems, Inc. The program presented three different influence styles: pull, push and move-away [11]. Each style has associated actions that the influencer can practice. A summary of the styles and their associated actions are shown on Slide #59. I found the system simple to follow and easy to practice.

Mastering Influence Styles

- Push style requires a lot of energy
    - Persuading: proposing; reasoning
    - Asserting: setting expectations; evaluating; using incentives and pressure
- Pull style requires less energy
    - Bridging: involving; listening; disclosing
    - Attracting: finding common ground; visioning
- Move-away style requires little energy
    - Disengaging: Postponing; processing; changing subject; taking a break
    - Avoiding

Source: Positive Power and Influence Program by Situation Management Systems, Inc.   Slide 59

The push style requires the influencer to use his or her power to press the issue in the preferred direction. As you practice this style, you feel like you are sitting in the driver seat and putting energy in driving the issue to resolution. This style consists of persuading and asserting actions. Persuading is further divided into proposing and reasoning. Proposing is putting your desired position in front of people as the preferred option. Examples of proposing statements are:

- I suggest _____.
- I propose _____.
- I recommend _____.
- I have an idea _____.
- What if we _____.

Reasoning is providing logic to motivate others to choose the option you like. Example of reasoning statements are:

- We should _____ because _____.
- The reason is _____ so you should _____.
- Let me explain why we need to _____.
- Let me give you an example _____.

Asserting is divided into setting expectations, evaluating, using incentives and pressure. Setting expectations is stating what you expect others to do. Examples of setting expectation statements are:

- I want _____.
- I need _____.
- We should _____.
- You must _____.

Evaluating is assessing people's actions or the situation caused by these actions. Through the assessment, communicate your preference for others to follow. Example of evaluating statements are:

- I like it when you _____.
- What we _____ is an excellent choice.
- I don't believe that is good when you _____.
- Doing _____ is inadequate.

Using incentives and pressure is straightforward, and the example statements are:

- If you _____ I will _____.
- If you don't _____ I will _____.
- Please do _____ or I will _____.

The pull style channels the power of influence targets to the preferred direction of the influencer. Using this influence style is similar to practicing Tai Chi, a form of martial arts that relies on the power of soft. It absorbs and redirects the energy of others to achieve the desired effect. This influence style includes bridging and attracting. Bridging is separated into involving, listening and disclosing. Involving is inviting others to join you to solve your issues. Examples of involving statements are:

- I need your help _____.
- I have a problem _____.
- Tell me more about _____.
- Help me understand your _____.
- I hear that _____.

Listening is practicing active listening by paraphrasing someone's statement as what you think is correct. Example of listening statements are:

- So, you are saying _____.
- If I understand you _____.
- It sounds like _____.

Disclosing is sharing information that you find useful to hint others to use the information or follow the actions you disclosed. Example of disclosing statements are:

- I have information for you _____.
- I know that in the past we _____.
- I have dealt with a problem _____.

Attracting is divided into finding common ground and visioning. Finding common ground is utilizing shared values to motivate others based on the social and belonging needs described in Maslow's needs theory. Example of finding common ground statements are:

- We all believe in _____.
- I think we all feel that _____.
- Together we can _____.
- What we have in common is _____.

Visioning is creating a picture of success to inspire others to contribute to making that success a reality, which is a powerful motivational approach advocated by many leadership theories. Example of visioning statements are:

- What I see us doing is _____.
- With your effort, the result will be _____.
- Imagine that _____.
- The future will be _____.
- Can you see what I see _____?

The move-away style uses disengagement and retention to draw others into the position desired by the influencer. When practicing this influence style, your energy is preserved while others' energy is building because people tend to really want things they can't get. The move-away style consists of disengaging and avoiding, but the *Positive Power and Influence* training program does not advocate the use of avoiding because it considers avoiding backing out and giving up. I disagree as most of us have experienced the power of silent treatment. Leonardo da Vinci once said, "Nothing strengthens authority so much as silence." Of course, you cannot use avoiding often, as this will be considered an immature behavior. Unlike avoiding, disengaging still requires action by the influencer to prevent others from taking actions that lead to undesirable outcome. It is divided into postponing, processing, changing subject and taking a break. Example of postponing statements are:

- Let's do _____ next.
- Why don't we push this out _____?
- Let's wait until we _____.
- Let me think about _____ and get back to you later.

Example of processing statements are:

- Let's get back to the agenda and _____.
- The procedure requires us to _____.

- Why don't we double check _____?
- We do not have much time so _____.

Example of changing subject statements are:

- Let's discuss _____ first.
- We need to hold this thought and move on to _____.
- Let's go back to the earlier idea _____.
- This reminds me that we need to consider _____.

Example of taking a break statements are:

- Let's take a break _____.
- We should stop talking _____ and think _____.
- Let's go back to the earlier idea _____.
- I need to take a break on _____ and get back to you.

These influence styles require practice and can yield different results with different people in different situations. The effectiveness of an influence act may depend on the personality type of the individual. You can find information about personality types from the Myers-Briggs Type Indicator (MBTI) [12] or the DiSC assessment [13]. However, unless you are their manager, you cannot simply request people to complete the survey or tell you their personality type. You need to sense the different personality types through your interfaces with them and act accordingly. Regardless, you need to master all three styles and use them based on the situation. You will see some general guidance on when to use which style when managing up, across and down at the workplace.

> How to manage up, across and down working relationships?

At a workplace, you have to manage the working relationships of three different groups of people: managers, peers and subordinates. Managing up is more critical than managing the other relationships, especially if you want to advance your career. The pull influence style is the most commonly used in managing up, specifically listening, disclosing and involving. Reasoning in the push style is also practiced when you have data to support your claim.

Before influencing your manager to act in your favor, you need to put yourself into his or her position and think logically as you were the manager. On several occasions, I have seen recently graduated employees propose new ideas that could save company money and headcount but were rejected by management. They came to my advising sessions and complained that their manager did not value their opinion and ideas. Some were even considering leaving their job. The reason their proposals were rejected was usually not because of the quality of the ideas, but because they did not see things from their managers' perspectives.

Managing Various Working Relationships

- Managing up
    - Use listening, disclosing, involving and reasoning
    - See things from your manager's perspective
    - Challenge wisely, show data and results
    - Be proactive
- Managing across
    - Use all influence styles
    - Create alliances
- Managing down
    - Use all influence styles
    - Practice situational leadership

Slide 60

Most managers have strong desires in growing their business. They also aggressively seek power as measured by the size of their organization and budgets. I told my advisees, as a manager, I could not impulsively accept cost and headcount saving proposals unless I could use the saved resources elsewhere. I joked that if they worked for me, my department would become smaller and need fewer employees, so logically I would let them go first because they caused this problem. In this particular situation, I suggested they consider including how to use the saved resources as part of their proposal.

There are many other cases where you and your manager's priorities are not aligned. If you want to influence someone, put yourself in their position first and understand their concerns. Sometimes you even need to think like the manager of your manager to maximize the benefits of a proposal. First line managers think differently from middle level managers, and executives also think differently from middle managers, because each management level has its unique challenges, priorities and concerns.

Even if you put yourself in your manager's position and think critically, you may still miss some key factors due to limits in views, experience and information available to you. Therefore, you need to be very careful about challenging upward. Missing key factors in your thinking process is only one aspect. Susceptibility of risks plays a more important role in upper management as the stakes are higher when choosing the wrong path. Don't blame your manager for being too conservative and unwilling to take risks. Your manager has the responsibility to ensure that any new approach is validated and implemented with extra care.

When you think you have a better solution and your manager does not agree, do not challenge back immediately. Collect additional data and walk through the thinking process again with your manager's concerns in mind. If possible, conduct a pilot experiment or make a prototype to demonstrate the results. You may also consider doing one version using your manager's approach and another using your approach, so that you can really experience both and prove which one is better. This means you need to put in extra time and effort, but this is what it takes to demonstrate your commitment and perseverance for better results. Don't challenge upward with words; instead, do it with actions, data and results.

Being proactive is another tactic in managing up. To do this, you first need to get to know your manager. You need to find information such as personality type, management style, pet peeves, hot buttons, communication preferences, etc. Such information can help you to understand your manager's expectations. We have already discussed how to exceed expectations in the task management session. You can also exceed your manager's expectations by proactively providing information and achieving results before your manager requests them. In order to do this, you should know your manager's schedule and routines. For example, if you are doing a project for a manager who has a meeting next week with an important client, you can prepare a project update and send it to the manager on Friday. This manager will most likely to be happy to see this message without asking. As a manager, I love to have such subordinates work for me.

To extend this further, you should find out all your manager's meetings over the next few weeks and see what you can provide for each meeting. Similarly, find out the deadlines of your manager's deliverables and complete your portion of the tasks ahead of time. How do you find out your manager's schedule? If your manager does not make it public, you need to find it through networking with your colleagues, starting with your manager's administrative assistant, who usually does the schedule for the manager.

Managing across requires you to master and use all influence styles. Assessment of the situation is important in determining which style to use. For colleagues who are senior to you and trusted by management, you should use the same styles as managing up. For other colleagues, a proposing statement is a popular choice along with disclosing and involving. Use the other influence styles occasionally as appropriate.

In addition, avoid the use of "I" in sentences whenever possible. In the influence statement examples shown earlier, there are many sentences that start with "I". Emphasizing "I" is fine when you communicate with your manager and senior people, which shows that you have confidence and take full responsibility for what you say. However, when working with peers, you should rephrase the statements to avoid "I". As many people have quoted, there is no "I" in team. For instance, replace "I recommend..." with "We could consider..." Use "We need..." instead of "I need..." Practice the influence actions and rephrase sentences based on the reactions from your colleagues.

Building alliances with your peers is important as you are unlikely to accomplish all your assignments alone. Not only do you need support and cooperation from your peers, having allies can also make you happier at work. There will be no alliance when trust is absent. To do this, you need to exhibit full professionalism. Do not participate in gossip or talk about your coworkers behind their back. Never back-stab or blind-side your peers. Communicate directly with your peers if there are issues. Do not escalate a problem up the management chain unless you give your colleague a chance to work the issue first. Show your commitment in team projects by putting in your best effort and be willing to take on extra administrative support to the team. Be dependable by keeping your promises and complete your tasks before deadlines. More importantly, be empathetic and considerate. Influence others with sensitivity and flexibility. "Don't do unto others what you don't want done unto you."

As your career progresses, you will become a senior member of the team or may even become a manager. You need to learn how to manage down, which means acquiring leadership skills. Since this career session is not designed for senior managers and executives, I will only cover a few key points to get new leaders started on the right track. Besides, becoming an effective leader requires a lot of training and cannot be covered by just one book anyway. Leadership is a key area in management and probably has the greatest number of theories in managerial studies.

As far as influence styles are concerned, all styles are applicable in managing down. When you are new to a leadership role, my recommendation is to use the pull styles primarily. As your position strengthens, you should consider applying the influence styles based on the situational leadership theories, which form a subset of leadership theories. There are many situational leadership theories. The popular ones are Fiedler's contingency model and the Least Preferred Co-worker

(LPC) theory developed from this model, Hersey and Blanchard's Situational Leadership theory, House's Path-Goal theory, and the Vroom-Yetton decision model. For starters, I recommend using Hersey and Blanchard's Situational Leadership theory.

The main contingency factor in Hersey and Blanchard's theory is follower readiness, which is divided into four levels based on the combination of follower ability and willingness or confidence [14]. Follower readiness level 1 (R1) is when the follower is unable and lacks motivation or confidence to perform. R2 is when the follower is unable but motivated or confident to perform. R3 is when the follower has the ability but is unwilling to use the ability or insecure to perform alone. R4 is when the follower has the ability, motivation and confidence to perform.

According to Hersey and Blanchard, the appropriate leadership style for R1 followers is telling. For R2, the suitable leadership style is selling. For R3, it is participating, and for R4, it is delegating. Based on these recommendations, we can utilize influence style actions that match the leadership style and follower readiness characteristics. For example, practicing the telling leadership style for R1 followers can use asserting, setting expectations and using incentive and pressure in the push influence style. Exercising participating leadership style for R3 followers primarily uses involving, disclosing and visioning in the pull influence style.

To become an effective leader, you need to spend a lot more effort to acquire leadership skills. It is a long journey, and as you move up, each step in the leadership ladder requires additional skills.

> How to improve your communication at the workplace?

Practicing influence requires strong communication skills, which is also fundamental to achieving great teamwork and collaboration. Communication is a huge topic with numerous methods, models and practices covered by countless books. I do not intend to make this writing an encyclopedia by reciting all the methods and models. My desire is to discuss the frequently used practices that address the most challenging situations at work.

Managing Professional Communication

- Micro-advantages and micro-inequity
    - Understand micro-messages sent by others and monitor micro-messages you send
- CREATOR meeting management
    - Send out meeting invite with CREA: Category, Roles, Expectations and Agenda
    - Execute the meeting with TOR: Timekeeping, Outcome and Record
- SMART reporting
    - Straightforward, Memorable, Action-oriented, Relevant, and Timely

Slide 61

> How to communicate effectively through non-verbal cues?

One of the major frustrations for people at work is the feeling of being misunderstood or not being understood at all. While we are feeling like victims in the fast-changing work environment and complaining that others do not communicate enough, we are doing the same to each other. We actually communicate far more information with hand gestures, facial expressions and tone of voice than through words. Many of us simply do not pay enough attention to these forms of communication. We unintentionally send out a great amount of micromessages through these non-verbal cues. In his book *Micromessaging: Why Great Leadership is Beyond Words*, Stephen Young points out that, "Developing the skill and language to identify and address negative micromessages puts a new power in your grasp... The new skill will enable you to rally everyone around you with micromessages that inspire, motivate, and get beyond conventional rhetoric [15]."

Negative micromessages are called microinequities. We need to minimize microinequities by being conscious of our facial expressions while interfacing with others. Most microinequities are communicated through facial expressions, which we cannot see ourselves. Many of us can sense signs of impatience, displeasure and absence, which cause us to feel disrespected. We then shut off or cease participating sincerely in return. We also need to monitor our personal greetings and interactions with others. Many people unconsciously show closeness to people who they like and are formal with the others. These signs can be easily sensed, and favoritism is perceived. Responding to differences of opinion is another situation where people easily send out unintentional micromessages. Slight overreaction and subtle signs of disparity are enough to make others feel uncomfortable. All of these microinequities lead to distrust in the work environment that make collaboration more difficult.

Positive micromessages are called microadvantages. To maximize microadvantages, we should first be truly immersed in the conversation through active listening and asking questions. Build rapport with others by sending micromessages that you are interested in them as a person not just the work performed by them. Proactively solicit opinions and at the same time send sincere micromessages that make others feel valued. In team discussions, acknowledge and address others using individuals' names instead of "he" or "her idea." When addressing a group, pay equal attention to every single person with routine eye contact from time to time. When being interrupted, calmly acknowledge the person speaking and politely shift the focus back to the original idea. To learn more about utilizing microadvantages, please read Young's book. Learning this skill can improve your emotional intelligence and enable you to discover the hidden needs and information of others.

> How to effectively manage meetings?

Another frustration for people at work is having too many meetings. Attending meetings is not a favorite activity for most employees. In fact, many people hate meetings and feel that they are a waste of time. According to research done by Rick Gilbert, an executive coach for many Fortune 500 companies such as Apple, Cisco, eBay and Oracle, executives consider that more than two-third of meetings are complete failures [16]. Igloo Software surveyed 1000 people and found that 76% of meetings are not necessary [17]. Another survey done by ResourcefulManager on 948 executives and managers indicated that almost half of meetings accomplish nothing [18]. If you set and run your meetings effectively or contribute to improving meetings hosted by others, you will be well liked and appreciated by the attendees.

I developed the CREATOR Meeting management system that helps to increase meeting effectiveness, and it was first published in my book *Project Management for Continuous Innovation* in 2019. CREATOR stands for Category, Roles, Expectations, Agenda, Timekeeping, Outcome and Record. CREA are recommended for the meeting invitation and TOR is used for how the meeting should be run [19].

First, the category of the meeting should be clear to attendees. Companies generally have common meeting categories that are understood by employees. For instance, in his book *High Output Management*, Intel former CEO Andy Grove categorized meetings into process-oriented meetings and mission-oriented meetings [20]. Process-oriented meetings are regular meetings including one-on-one, staff and operational review meetings. Mission oriented meetings are ad-hoc meetings for problem-solving and decision-making.

In general, meetings can be categorized as action, status update, information sharing, decision-making, problem-solving, innovation and team-building meetings. It does not matter how meetings are categorized: the important thing is to name them intuitively so that they can be understood by most people, and then have a standard CREA template for each category of meetings. This will make your meeting invitations more consistent and easier to read. It will also save time by reusing the template for future meetings in the same category.

Clear roles need to be defined so participants can be prepared before a meeting so as to not waste time during the meeting figuring out who is doing what. Having clearly documented expectations for the participants is important to ensure the meeting is focused and runs like clockwork.

An agenda is super critical for meetings as a large percentage of meetings ineffectively manage time. The survey done by ResourcefulManager shows about 40% of meetings do not end on time [18]. Agenda items must have time allocations as well as owners, so that meeting participants know what is expected from them.

CREATOR Meeting Management

Subject: ABC Task Force Kick-off Meeting
Category: Action Meeting
Roles: Facilitator: Lily
          Timekeeper: Ava
          Note-taker: Leo
          Decision Maker: Dan
          Required Participants: Ella, Jack, Nora, Mike, May
Expectations: - Tasks assigned to all team member
                   - Preliminary schedule defined
Agenda: 8:00 – Overall task force objective, Dan
           8:10 – Task requirements, Lily facilitate/All contribute
           8:30 – Task assignment, All
           8:40 – Tentative schedule, Lily/All
           8:55 – Open items, All

During meeting: T=Timekeeping, O=Outcome, R=Record

Slide 62

Meeting invitations with CREA should be sent to all meeting participants ahead of time along with a time and place in the email scheduling tool used by your company. An example of an action meeting invitation is shown on Slide #62. The best time to send meeting invitations depends on the category of the meeting and the time required for participants to get prepared.

The TOR part of the CREATOR Meeting system applies when meetings are actually in session. T stands for timekeeping, which is extremely important for keeping a meeting on track and productive, otherwise the agenda is just a wish list. This key responsibility belongs to the timekeeper who should highlight how much time the presenters have before each time slot and remind them when their time is near the end. Pick a disciplined individual as the timekeeper for your meeting or do it yourself. Timekeepers may use typical sentences such as: "Ella and Mike, you are up and have 15 minutes." "Five minutes remaining." "You only have a couple minutes, please wrap it up."

O stands for outcome, which is another dimension that is critical for running an effective meeting. If we do not get results from the agenda items, discussing them is a waste of time. Keeping focus on the outcome of the agenda items is the responsibility of the facilitator who should ensure a focused discussion with high quality conversations. When there are conflicts and disagreements, the facilitator needs to redirect the discussion back to the topic at hand, so the meeting does not go down a rabbit hole.

When people are passive and unwilling to contribute, the facilitator needs to promote group discussion and encourage members to share ideas. Essentially, the facilitator's role is to ask for facts, opinions and suggestions to ensure the discussion yields the best possible outcome.

If you are running the meeting, it is possible for you to be both the timekeeper and facilitator. Facilitators may ask these typical questions:

- "What are we intending to achieve?"
- "What is the meaning of this?"
- "What data supports your claim?"
- "How can we do this effectively?"
- "Mike, what do you think about this idea?"

R stands for record, which should capture the key points of the discussions and in many cases, the decisions and actions that need to be executed after the meeting. Many people refer to this record as meeting minutes. The note-taker has this responsibility. Proper record of the meeting drives attendance and actions as well as serves as the proof of agreement. Meeting records should be short and simple but also need to capture all the key information and actions needed to be performed. Using a staff meeting as an example, the meeting record may look like what is shown on the next page.

In addition, meeting records should be produced in a timely manner. In fact, it would be best to have the note-taker doing it while the meeting is in progress so that it is done when the meeting ends. Writing the record online or using tools such as Microsoft SharePoint and Google Docs allow all the members to see the document as it is being updated so that any errors can be spotted and corrected real time.

To further improve the effectiveness of certain meetings, the following ground rules may be useful:

- Attendance is not required if any part of CREA is missing in the meeting invite.
- Attendees may attend only the agenda slots that are assigned or of interested.

- Cancel and reschedule the meeting when key roles are absent, or more than half of participants decline.

Staff Meeting Dec. 5, 2017

Attendance: (P - Present, E - Excused, A - Absent)

	WW43	WW44	WW45	WW46	WW47	WW48	WW49	WW50	WW51
Dan	P	P	P	P	P	E	P		
Lily	P	P	P	P	P	P	P		
Ava	P	P	E	P	P	P	P		
Leo	P	E	P	P	P	P	P		
Ella	P	P	P	P	P	P	P		
Jack	P	P	A	P	P	A	P		
Nora	P	P	P	P	P	E	P		
Mike	E	P	P	A	P	P	P		
May	P	P	P	P	P	E	P		

Discussion Summary: (i. - FYI, a. Action required)

- Safety and urgent issues, John/All
    i. Site building shutdown for maintenance on WW50 weekend.
    a. Potential chemical leak identified in equipment C. Need to check all existing tools by WW50 – Leo.

- Project A update, Ella/Mike
    i. Project A progress is on track for completion Q1 next year.
    a. Report out budget spending status in WW51 meeting – Mike.

- Project B proposal, Jack
    i. Project B will improve current market position and attract new customers.
    a. Based on the current proposal, Project B requires about 50% more resources than project A. Inform finance department by the end of this week – Dan.

- Project C requirements, Lily/Ava
    i. 80% requirements are collected and 20% pending. Expected to complete WW51.
    a. Need to double check with customer A to fully understand requirement B. WW51 - Lily

- Opens, All
    i. A cost reduction proposal is being worked by team A. Will bring it to this meeting when ready. Completion date yet to be determined.
    a. Customer B request information on Product C. Need to check with legal department for IP release. WW52 – Ella.

Action Items:

Task	Owner	Done By	Description	Status
49.1	Leo	WW50	Check all tools for chemical leak	
49.2	Mike	WW51	Report out Project A budget spending status	
49.3	Dan	WW49	Inform finance on Project B resource requirement	
49.4	Lily	WW51	Check with customer A on project C requirement B	
49.5	Ella	WW52	Check with legal for IP release on Product C	

Teleconferences are conducted more frequently in recent years due to the increase of global teams and reduction of travel budgets. The

CREATOR Meeting system can easily be applied to manage teleconferences by just adding expectations such as announcing yourself before speaking, putting on mute when not speaking, avoiding background noises and no multitasking.

> How to write a good report?

Besides meetings, report writing is another activity that many people are not thrilled to do but critical for communicating and learning. Many have probably heard of SMART goal setting, which was coined by George Doran in 1981 and later modified by many others using different words to make up the acronym SMART [21]. The original five words were Specific, Measurable, Assignable, Realistic and Time-related. I adapted the term SMART and developed the SMART reporting with these different words: Straightforward, Memorable, Action-oriented, Relevant and Timely [19].

Straightforward means communicating points in a succinct and direct fashion. On written reports, key messages should be stated in the first few sentences. Having a summary section in the beginning is also helpful. You can even label it as "Key Messages." For verbal reports, key messages should be in the first slide of the PowerPoint right after the title page or even on the title page. Tell the audience what you are going to tell them, what the important points of your presentation are and then support them with data.

One of my habits is that when I am asked to present a report in a certain length of time, I will develop a version that takes half of the time and another version that takes three quarters of the time. It forces me to be concise and prioritize materials. It is typical that most presentations go over their scheduled time, and in cases when you present the half-time version of the report, you will have the appreciation of meeting participants, especially the chair of the meeting. In a way, your presentation stands out. Under normal circumstances, present the three-quarter version so that time is well managed. There may be some uncontrolled events that take extra time, such as people asking too many questions. If you are on time and no one asks any question, you can summarize the key points at the end, so the key messages really stand out for the audience. By the way, the two versions can be built in a single PowerPoint file. All you need to do is to use special marks and graphics on the items that you would skip when doing the short version.

Memorable means making your report standout and impressing your target audience so that they remember what you present. Develop your report from the viewpoint of the audience and make it enjoyable for them by creating an emotional connection with them. Make the presentation more interesting by using visuals but do so wisely. Pay attention to details and do not use hard to read text, bullet points or charts.

Action-oriented means clearly stating what you want your target audience to do and/or what you are going to do. Maximize the value of your report and that value is from actions but not just words on paper. Being a manager for many years, one of my top dislikes is that people report issues without actions, so I have to ask, "What would you like me to do or what are you going to do about it?" Even if the report is all about good news, there can still be some possible actions such as recognizing the team and sharing knowledge across the company.

Relevant means presenting the right information to the right audience. Get the context before you present so you know what your audience cares about. Presenting too much information will overwhelm the audience and cloud the key messages. Too little information will not be convincing enough to establish credibility. Usability is the key measurement for the relevance of a report. The information presented must be useful for the audience, so think about how the content of the report can be utilized when developing it.

Timely means delivering or presenting the report at the right time. Delayed reports delay actions. In some cases, management and clients usually prefer to have access to the task progress in real time, so for written status reports, it would be best to create real-time reports that users can access at the time of need or automate these reports so that users can subscribe and have them sent via email regularly. You should consider doing an oral presentation after an occurrence of a major event, whether it is a planned milestone or an unplanned problem. Keeping the visibility of key accomplishments and issues is important for you to stand out, showing ownership and control of the situation, especially in large corporations. It is out of sight, out of mind. If you are not visible, you are at risk of losing your job.

How to prepare for and deal with difficult situations?

So far, we have gone through the key aspects of selecting and improving your work environment, namely choosing a company with good corporate policies and physical environment, developing professional relations and managing communication. The practices discussed are for normal circumstances. Problems are inevitable, and you better be prepared. When a crisis occurs, you can stay calm to solve the problem and be able to make the best decisions in a stressful environment. Having predefined problem-solving and decision-making processes will make things easier for you in unsettling situations.

Managing Difficult Situations

- Problems are inevitable and you better be prepared by defining processes to deal with them
- Convergent problem-solving
    - Improve reality
    - Manage expectations
- "It is in your moments of decision that your destiny is shaped." - Tony Robbins
- The difficulty of making a decision is that you cannot have everything, you must compromise
- Six-step decision-making process: timing, framing, aiming, forming, affirming and performing

Slide 63

How to solve a problem effectively?

Having problems is not entirely negative. If we are doing challenging work, problems are expected. Therefore, we should have a predefined process for addressing problems, so when a problem surfaces, you will not be surprised and can act calmly to solve it. A problem exists when the reality is different from the expectation. The bigger the gap means the bigger the problem. To solve a problem means closing the gap between reality and expectation. Most people solve problems by improving the reality. It is more effective, however, to solve problems by working from both ends: improving the reality and changing the expectation. Based on my experience, the Convergent Problem-solving model was developed and is shown on Slide #64 [19].

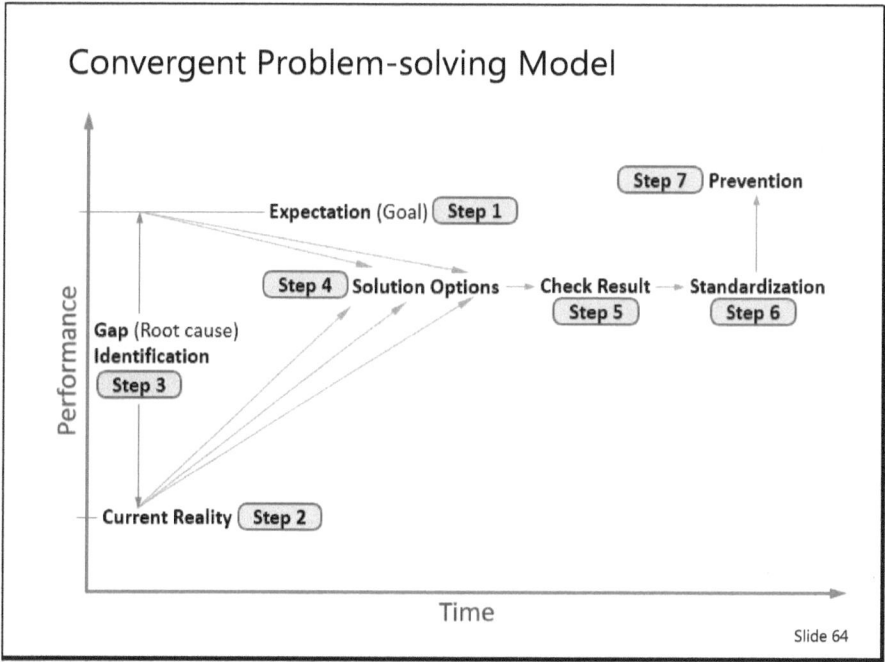

Step 1 of the model is to fully understand the performance expectations. This is the successful ideal state that will satisfy all stakeholders. Therefore, this is the performance goal that you are shooting for originally.

Since you have a problem, you need to understand the current reality, which is the situation that we are in now. A problem exists when the situation is not ideal for some or all stakeholders, so Step 2 is to understand the current situation. If you do not know where you are, it is difficult to find the path to where you want to be.

Step 3 is to identify the gap and root causes that lead to the gap between the current state and the expected ideal state. Tools such as the fishbone diagram and failure mode and effects analysis (FMEA) are useful for this step.

Step 4 is to formulate options for closing the gap, which should be looking from both the goal and the current reality perspectives. You can brainstorm using the Convergent Problem-solving Solution Generation Flow shown on Slide #65.

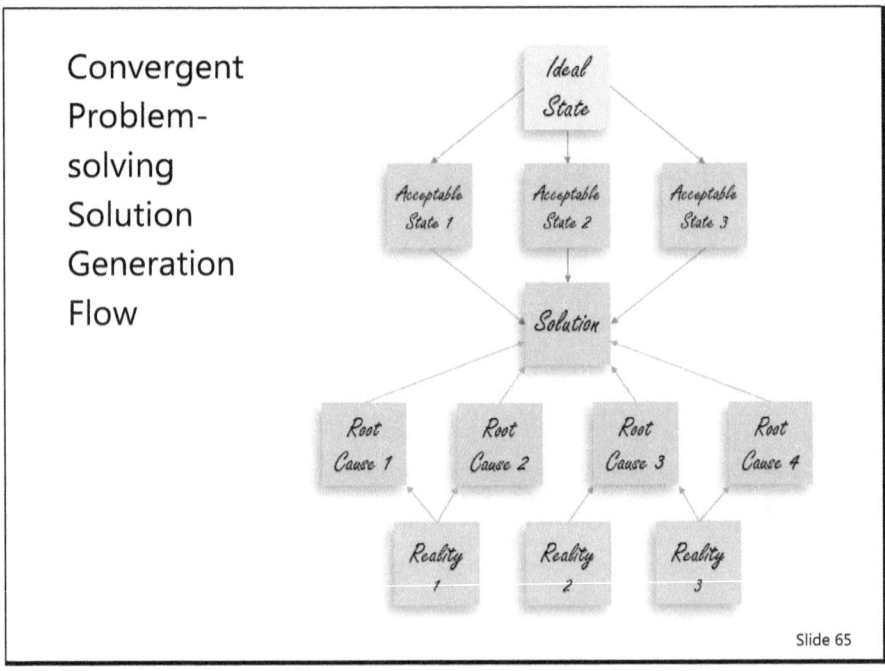

Slide 65

From the top-down direction, you need to work with the stakeholders or management to define acceptable states, which may be less desirable than the ideal state. It is a process of re-examining the feasibility and achievability of the original ideal state and prioritizing resources for the best-case scenario under the current constraints. From the bottom-up direction, a typical problem-solving approach applies: identifying the root causes of the issues and addressing those causes. When developing solutions, you also need think about the time scale, which means developing short-term, medium-term and long-term solutions to the problem.

Step 5 is to put the selected solutions into action and check to see if these solutions are truly getting you to an acceptable state. Many problem-solving models end with this step. However, if you want to be proactive in addressing similar problems in the future, you need to take this further.

Step 6, which is to standardize the solutions so that the process can be readily applied should the problem occur again. This step is especially beneficial if you are working for a large corporation, as the problem is likely to happen at a different place and/or at a future time. Having a standard for solving certain problems will allow you to solve these problems quickly and consistently. You can also share the standard solution with your colleagues to increase your visibility and value to your company.

You can also take one additional step to Step 7, which is to learn from all the previous steps and come up with measures that prevent similar problems from ever happening again. Doing this step correctly eliminates the need for the standards created in Step 6 and possibly even eliminates the need for using this problem-solving model for the problem. This takes the performance to the next level, as it would typically exceed the expectations of the stakeholders and management by stopping problems before they occur.

How to make the right decision?

Time and time again, there are different paths in front of us, and we need to decide which way to go. These may be critical moments that change our lives. Author Tony Robbins wrote, "It is in your moments of decision that your destiny is shaped." Decision-making determines which option is the best to pursue. If we could do everything we wanted to do and had everything we wanted to have, decision-making would be simple. Most of us, however, are living in a world with limited resources, so we have to make choices to do certain things while simultaneously giving something up.

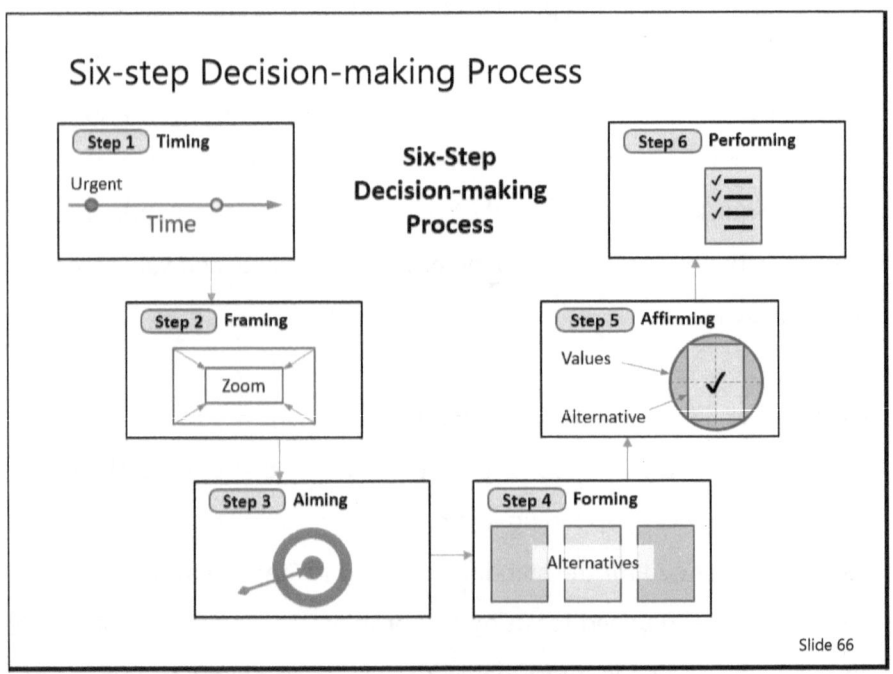

How can we make better decisions? Shown on Slide #66, I developed a six-step decision-making process, which provides a general step-by-step guide for individuals and organizations to make better decisions. The Six-step Decision-making process consists of the timing, framing, aiming, forming, affirming and performing steps.

The timing step is to determine the urgency of a decision. Some decisions only have a small window of opportunity and the consequences will be significant if you miss this window. People who are considered indecisive are in essence missing the best timing to make a decision. There will always be additional useful information that you can collect for a given decision. When to stop collecting data therefore depends on the urgency of the decision. Determining the timing for the decision is the first step, as it defines the subsequent actions in making the decision. A decision that needs to be made today will require a different course of action from a decision that can be made next month. Making a fire-fighting decision in reaction to an urgent request, for instance, is much different than making a planning decision for a project starting next quarter.

Framing a decision is the second step, which involves defining the scope of a decision. Framing a decision to broadly may overwhelm you such that you are unable to pinpoint the right issue. Framing a decision too narrowly will lead to missing threats and opportunities. The best illustration for framing a decision is shown on Slide #67. Obviously, a bad frame limits your view and prevents you from making the best choice. You need to zoom in and out while analyzing the situation to find the right assumptions for the decision.

The third step is aiming, which means setting the general direction for a decision. When you are in a situation where you are not satisfied, there are only three general directions available: change it, accept it or leave it. You should consider making the choice in that order as well. The first choice is to determine what you can do to change the situation. If you can, then the decision is to seek possible actions that alter the circumstances in your favor. If you determine that you cannot change the situation, which is true in many cases, then your next choice is to accept it and then find ways to minimize the impact. You cannot stop the rain, but you can use an umbrella.

Sometimes at work, you are asked to disagree and commit. It means that you need to accept an undesirable fact and work with it. Lastly, if you find that you cannot accept a situation, which you cannot change, then the last option is to leave. Aiming is a key step for many personal decisions, such as working on an undesirable job or living with an undesirable relationship. The first attempt is to change the situation. If you cannot, then ask yourself if you can accept it. If you cannot do that either, then the only choice left is to leave.

Once the general direction is determined, we can move to the fourth step, which is forming alternatives. Alternatives are the options that can be acted upon and within your power and control. Typically, you need to come up with at least three alternatives. Brainstorming and Brainswarming are tools that can be used to develop alternatives. If none of your alternatives looks good to you, get ideas from people who you trust. Do not confuse alternatives with goals and outcomes. They are possible course of actions that are available to you. Good alternatives are potentially attractive from at least one aspect, significantly different and under your control.

Decision Matrix Template

- Generate criteria that you value
- Assign weight factors to the criteria
- Score each alternative
- Consider the highest score alternative as your final decision

	Criteria 1	Criteria 2	Criteria 3	Criteria 4	Criteria 5	Total Score
Weight Factor	1X	3X	1X	3X	5X	
Alternative A						
Alternative B						
Alternative C						

Slide 68

The fifth step is selecting an alternative that aligns with your values. A decision matrix with alternatives against selection criteria could be used. An example of a decision matrix template is shown on Slide #68. The criteria should be aligned to your desires and values. Since each criterion may carry a different value to you, a weight factor can be used to calculate the score for each alternative. The best option to act upon is the one with the highest total scores. By doing so, you have made a data-driven decision.

The final step is acting on the chosen alternative and following through the decision. A decision that is not being acted on is merely a wish. You can make everything look pretty in PowerPoint slides showing step one to five but without actions, no value is created. If you are halfhearted about your commitment to the decision, your follow through is usually less intense and may not achieve the best results.

Session 5 Summary: Managing Your Environment

- You have ownership over your work environment
- Choose to work for a company with good corporate policies and enjoyable physical environment
- Build and maintain your professional network for mutual benefits
- Master the push, pull and move-away influence styles
- Manage up, Across and down appropriately
- Improve communication by paying attention to micromessages, meeting management and reporting
- Handle difficult situations using predefined problem-solving and decision-making processes

Slide 69

In summary, a good work environment does not happen by chance. You have ownership and control over your work environment. First, work for company that has corporate policies that you agree and physical environment that you enjoy. Second, build your internal and external professional network with clear targets and priorities. Third, maintain professional relations with the right interactions and mutual benefits. Fourth, master influence styles and apply them situationally to get desirable results. Fifth, take the appropriate actions in managing up, across and down. Sixth, improve communication by sensing and using micromessages, conducting effective meetings and producing SMART reports. Lastly, stay calm and handle difficult situations through predefined problem-solving and decision-making processes.

Going through the last five sessions, I hope that you have learned something new, and at the same time, also gain the feeling that there is lot of information I have not touch. Indeed, there is still much to learn, and continuing education is essential to career success. In the next session, I will share the lessons that I learned from obtaining multiple graduate degrees, including doctorate in both engineering and business. I hope these lessons help you to become a better learner.

Session 5 Exercise #1 – Plan for networking

Step 1. Identify internal networking targets

Networking objective: _____

List the potential black and green dots: (Start from your company org. chart)

Individual/Position	Color Dot	Connecting Means
	Black	

Step 2. Identify external networking opportunities

List the networking events you consider going:
(Within in the next quarter, update every quarter)

#1 _____ Date and time: _____

    Place: _____

#2 _____ Date and time: _____

    Place: _____

#3 _____ Date and time: _____

    Place: _____

#4 _____ Date and time: _____

    Place: _____

Step 3. Identify external networking targets

List the potential black, green and key blue dots:
(State your intention with target)

Individual/Position	Color Dot	Networking Intention
	Black	

Step 4. Record monthly networking Journal

Month _____ networking meeting:
(Record the meeting date, short note and the next check date)

Individual/Position	Date	Note & Next Check Date

Session 5 Exercise #2 – Solve a problem

Use the Convergent Problem-solving template if you have a problem

Problem: _____

Ideal State (1)		

Acceptable State (4b)		
#1	#2	#3

Solution (5-7)		
(6) Procedure for future use? ☐		(7) Prevention actions? ☐

Possible Measures to Resolve Root Causes (4a)		
#1	#2	#3

Root Causes (3)		
#1	#2	#3

Current Reality (2)		

Session 5 Exercise #3 – Make a decision

Use the Six-step decision-making template if a decision is needed

Step 1. Determine the urgency and timing of the decision

Decision: _____

Timing	
Urgent? ☐	Decision deadline:

Step 2. Frame the decision by looking from different perspectives

Framing		
Short-term impact	Mid-term impact	Long-term impact

Step 3. Identify and set the general direction

Aiming		
Change	Accept	Leave
Pros	Pros	Pros
Cons	Cons	Cons

Circle the choice of direction after completing the por-con analysis

Step 4. Form alternatives under the general direction

Forming		
Alternative #1	Alternative #2	Alternative #3

Step 5. Rate the alternatives against your values

Affirming				
Your values	Weight	Alternative#1	Alternative#2	Alternative#3
	Total score			

Circle the highest score alternative as your decision

Step 6. Execute your decision using a checklist

Performing			
Actions	Date	Cautions	Done
			☐
			☐
			☐
			☐
			☐
			☐
			☐

Session 6

Learning and Education

Continue to learn and grow

> ## Session 6: Learning and Education
>
> "Intellectual growth should commence at birth and cease only at death." - Albert Einstein
>
> *Continuing education*
> - "Education is the passport to the future; for tomorrow belongs to those who prepare for it today" - Malcolm X
>
> *Learning how to learn*
> - "It is important that we discover an educational method where people learn to learn and go on learning their whole lives." - Rudolf Steiner
>
> *Becoming an expert*
> - "The top expert in the world are ardent students."
>   - Brendon Burchard
>
> Slide 71

> Why is continuous learning important?

From the TOP model as we discussed in the first session, learning enlarges your talent circle and therefore increases your chance of getting the dream job. In addition, the more skills you have, the better you can prepare for uncertainties and unexpected events. For instance, in the current COVID-19 pandemic, people with online tool skills can effectively shift their jobs into remote working from home. Furthermore, continuous learning can exercise your mind and enable you to explore beyond your limits, thereby bringing you a healthy and fulfilling life. As Henry Ford said, "Anyone who stops learning is old, whether at twenty or eighty. Anyone who keeps learning stays young." Albert Einstein also said, "Intellectual growth should commence at birth and cease only at death." Having a growth mindset is super important.

Learning reduces fear and encourages risk-taking, which is one of the key attributes of creativity and innovation. As demonstrated on Slide #72, everyone has a comfort zone and a fear zone. Personal development means reducing both the comfort zone and the fear zone to widen the learning zone. It is intuitive that learning can reduce fear, because the more you know, the greater control you have over the unknown, which is demonstrated in child development.

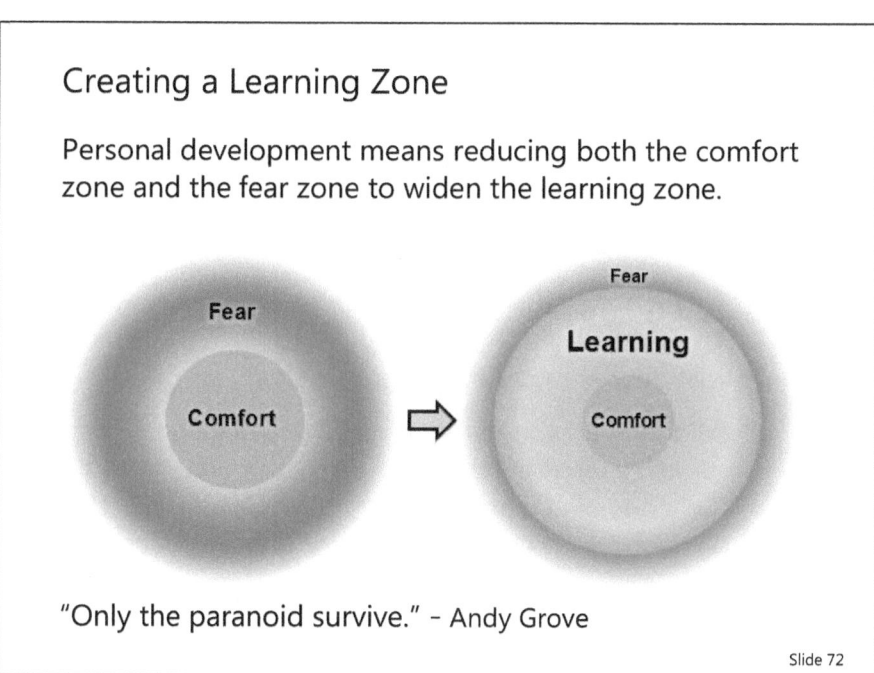

Slide 72

How does learning reduce the comfort zone? It is because the more you know, the more you know what you don't know. Once you get out of your comfort zone and look at the situation from a different angle, you will learn that what you believed to be safe before was often just a false sense of security. That is why Intel's former CEO and Chairman Andy Grove said, "Only the paranoid survive," and then used this phrase as the title of his book. Learning is therefore for both growth and survival.

> What are the means of continuing education?

Learning should not be a reactive activity. Being forced to learn new skills after being laid off will put you in a bad situation. In order to better control your career, or even life, you need to plan your education throughout your career. At the strategic level, what you need to learn has already been covered in Session 2, where skill requirements are mapped along the learning axis of your career plan template. Here, we will discuss the tactical plan for learning the chosen skills, which is about choosing learning methods. I will suggest several methods and you can use them individually or in combination.

Continuing Education

- Formal degree or certificate program
    - Working and studying in parallel: a place to practice learning, plus company supports
    - Self-discipline and sense of accomplishment
    - Broaden your horizons and new opportunities
- Open university courses - good trial with similar learning experience but less commitment
- Online courses - only suitable for learning technical skills that can be performed individually
- Corporate university courses - easy and accessible
- Personal coach - in-depth practical learning

Slide 73

My first suggestion is to enroll in a formal program, whether it is a graduate program or a certificate program. Of course, learning the time management skills in making time is a prerequisite as we discussed in

Session 3. Many universities and colleges offer early morning and evening classes for working professionals. Many companies also support their employees in continuing education by providing tuition reimbursement as well as flexible schedule for taking courses. I do not recommend taking a break from work to get a degree full time. Working and studying in parallel allows you to practice the learning and also utilize the support provided by your company. In addition, studying breaks up your work routine and makes your life more colorful by learning new things and meeting new people.

Indeed, completing a program while working takes commitment, but because it sets concrete targets that you are looking forward to achieving, it creates self-discipline to push yourself to complete the program. The sense of accomplishment may be a huge motivator as well. Over the long run, college degrees are depreciating just like our currencies. A century ago, having a college degree was prestigious. Now, a college degree is more like a high school diploma of that time, which was the minimum requirement for a decent job. Getting a degree or a certificate is an investment for the future. Therefore, if you are already putting the effort to learn the skills, getting a formal degree or a certificate at the same time would not be a bad idea.

It may require additional administrative effort and taking unplanned courses, but it is worth doing so. Taking additional courses should not be a waste, as you may gain knowledge that has unexpected impacts. For example, a calligraphy class that Steve Jobs audited in college turned out to be a significant inspiration for product development. You may gain new ideas or develop new perspectives on life, thereby broadening your horizons and discovering new opportunities.

If you are not yet ready to commit to a formal program, you can try the open university option first. Many universities and college offer courses that are open to anyone without an extensive application process for formal programs. For example, in the San Francisco Bay Area, University of California campus such as Berkeley and Santa Cruz both offer UC Extension courses. Stanford has the Continuing Studies Program. In the California State University system, San Francisco State University has the College of Extended Education. San Jose State University has the Open University department under the College of Professional and Global Education. Even community colleges, such as City College of San Francisco, College of San Mateo, and De Anza college all offer extension courses. You can check with universities and colleges in your area.

The open university courses are usually taught by the same faculty of the formal programs, so you are getting the same knowledge and similar experience as the formal courses. You may also be able to apply some of the course credits toward a formal program when you decide to pursue one in the future. If you select extension courses from reputable universities and colleges, many companies still provide tuition reimbursement as they do in formal programs. It may even be easier to get approval from management as the cost is lower.

Online learning is a popular means for continuing education, and it becomes even more popular now when we are in the midst of the COVID-19 pandemic. Online learning includes taking the pre-recorded courses offered by online learning platforms such as Coursera, MIT OpenCourseWare and Khan Academy, as well as online instructor led courses offered by universities and colleges. For certain subjects, especially those related to technical skills such as programming, online courses offer the convenience and flexibility. However, online courses are not ideal for learning skills that require frequent exchange of ideas or hands-on guidance. I am now teaching several courses at Santa Clara University and Stanford online through ZOOM due to the COVID-19 Stay at Home order. ZOOM has many collaboration features, so in theory, we can have an interactive class. But in reality, student-instructor interaction is much less despite my encouragement to the students to speak up. Student-student interaction is very rare. Many students are reluctant to turn on the video feature. My inexperience in online teaching may have caused some of these issues, but my peers have shared similar experiences. There are definitely shortcomings due to lack of face-to-face interaction. As mentioned in the previous session, taking courses can help you build a professional network, but doing it online is far less effective than doing it in person. The bottom line is to avoid taking online courses except for learning a technical skill that can be performed individually.

Another easy and accessible learning channel is through corporate universities. Many corporations understand that employee training is essential for building a learning organization. They establish corporate universities to provide courses for their employees and for customers as well. I have taken well over a hundred courses offered by my company, from technical skills such as HTML and java programming to business development and management such as the power and influence program mentioned in previous session. These courses are paid by the company and conducted on company time, which means you are paid while learning new skills that improve your employability. All you need to do is pay attention to the course offerings and practice your influence skills to convince your manager to let you take them. For those who do not work in a large company with a corporate university, you can still take courses offered by other companies. I have taken courses from Microsoft, Hewlett-Packard, Autodesk and Oracle. If these courses can significantly improve work productivity, and you can show the benefits of such a small investment, then I don't see why your manager will reject the proposal. As a manager for more than 30 years, I can tell you that such requests are rare, so if you demonstrate strong desires and confidence to achieve efficiency, then your chance of getting approval is very likely. Some departments have training budgets, and training credits also come with product purchases. If you don't ask, these opportunities will slip away.

Lastly, finding a personal coach is another potent way I recommend for continuing education. In old times, especially in Asian countries, key knowledge was imparted from expert masters to their loyal students. Following a master was the only way to learn certain secret skills. In modern times, people who compete in sports, music and pageants usually use personal trainers. In similar fashion, when you have a targeted learning area, you can identify the experts in this area, and then find one to be your personal coach and mentor. To be effective, you need to develop a deep relationship with this expert so that mutual trust is established. As such you will gain in-depth knowledge through one-on-one hands-on training.

Some people may ask how about learning by reading books, journals, etc. Reading alone is insufficient for learning many subjects. I consider reading as a subset of the methods mentioned above. It is rare that you are not required to read when taking courses. Even conventional courses based on lecture style instruction are often ineffective. As

Benjamin Franklin put it, "Tell me and I forget. Teach me and I remember. Involve me and I learn." You cannot always rely on the instructors to design interactive classes to involve you. You need to take actions to immerse yourself in learning, which means learning how to learn.

> What are the different levels of learning?

There are different levels of learning. Shown on Slide #74, Chris Argyris and Donald Schon developed a learning theory with the concept of single-loop, double-loop and triple-loop learning [22]. Single-loop learning is about learning the rules and the outcome of the learning is knowing how to follow the rules. Let's use teaching children addition: 1+1=2, as an example. Learning is completed once they memorize it and are able to do it again without mistakes.

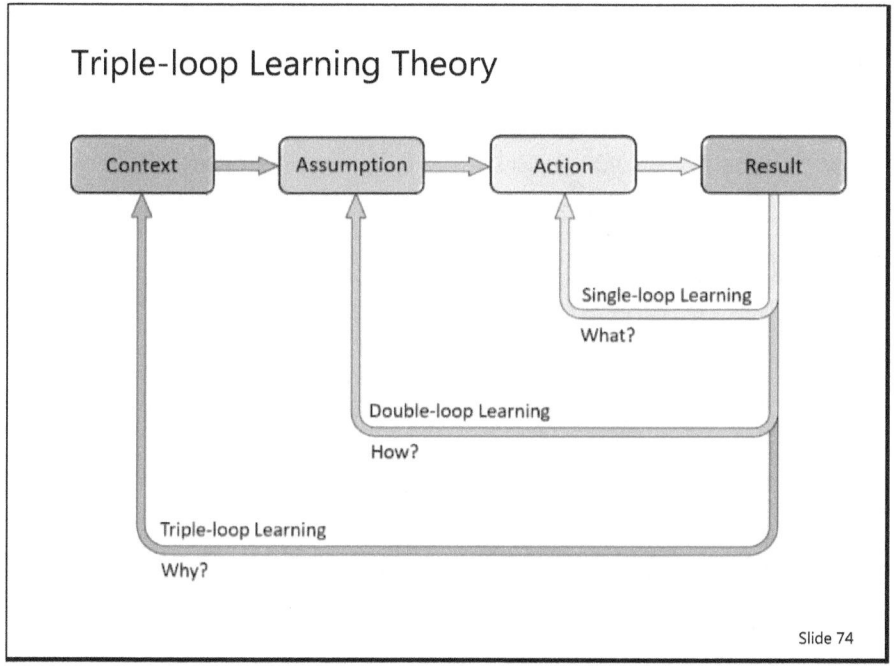

Double-loop learning is about learning to modify the rules and apply them appropriately. Continuing with the above example, double-loop learning is demonstrated by the children who now can do all simple additions, such as 1+1+1=3, 1+2=3, etc.

Triple-loop learning is about learning the rules themselves and the context of the rules. It is also referred as "learning how to learn." In the same example, we could ask the children to cite a real-life incidence of 1+1=2. They probably show adding one pencil to another pencil becomes two pencils. Now, what if we put a feeder fish in a fish tank with an Oscar fish, are we going to have two fishes eventually? Most likely the Oscar fish will eat the feeder fish and only one fish ends up in the tank. In this case, 1+1=1. In another case, what happens if we drop one drop of water on top of another drop of water. Do we have two drops of water? Again, we have 1+1=1. In a different situation, mom and dad got together to form a family and maybe ended up with a family of three or more if they have children. After exploring the different circumstances, the children will truly master the concept of addition and understand the conditions regarding when it works or when it doesn't work. Obviously, triple-loop learning often requires life experiences beyond just knowing the concepts, so it is seldom seen in classroom training.

Taking courses is still the primary channel for education. However, our current education system focuses on curriculum development, and the instructors determine the course content they believe students need. It is about what to learn, not how to learn. It makes the triple-loop learning largely dependent on you. You must engage in critical thinking and hands-on practices beyond course work and reading. I will share my view on the current education system, and then provide some suggestions on how to prepare yourself for the triple-loop learning under the current system.

> What exactly is education?

While most people agree that education is important, some people disagree on how education should be conducted and what a good education system looks like. For some people, education means formal schooling, which is phase in life and ends with graduation. After employment, going to school is called "Continuing Education" or "Extended Learning." For me and many others, it extends to life experiences beyond schooling and lasts a lifetime. Broadly speaking, education is just the process of imparting knowledge to individuals.

People often compare the education systems of the East and the West. The general view is that the education system of the East is too rigid and impedes creativity. On the other hand, the education system of the West lacks common standards, students play too much, and school time is not used effectively. Regardless of the main differences, both education systems are similar in the process of curriculum development. That is, education institutions and instructors decide what to teach and how to teach. They rely on experienced educators to determine what and how knowledge is being taught, based on the assumption that knowledge recipients are unknowledgeable, unaware what is the best for them, and prone to make mistakes.

Teaching content is the top priority of most instructors and motivating students to learn is secondary. In fact, many instructors consider themselves to be gatekeepers and believe that students who can pass the most rigorous scrutiny are the best students. Tough assignments, difficult exams, and grading on curves are common practices. They rarely consider student enjoyment when designing courses. To most students, finishing school is a relief. Parents are not helping either. Some parents push their children so hard that their children are stressed out and run out of motivation for continuing education. Others, on the contrary, let their children do what they like and do not encourage them to continue. I have seen that many students got frustrated in college and never want to go to school again.

After over 30 years of formal school studies, from kindergarten to multiple doctorate degrees, I found that the greatest value of education is not from the content that is taught. Only a small percentage of what we learned in school is useful in real life. After teaching at Silicon Valley universities for twenty years, I am more than certain that teaching content should not be the focus of education. Many educators may disagree with me, and my intention is by no means to disparage their contribution in curriculum development. In higher education specialty courses, the knowledge learned usually lags behind the knowledge currently used in the industry. Many universities hire adjuncts who are working in the industry to bring more practical contents to the students. However, due to the intellectual property protection of the adjuncts' companies, students still have no access to the latest and greatest unless they work in the industry as well. This is why I recommend working and doing graduate courses in parallel. Most students still need practical learning when getting to the workplace. Depending on the dynamics of the industry, there may be a lot of new content to learn.

In the case of foundational courses like math and physics, some people may argue that teaching content is very important. However, in today's digital world, we can easily find basic information online, and today's computers can do most of the calculations taught in these courses. Einstein said: "Never memorize something that you can look up." Do we really need to require our students to memorize the formulas and demonstrate step-by-step calculations within the limited exam time? When most courses in our education system are designed in such unenjoyable manner, I cannot see how most students are looking forward to doing this again. Based on a study done by Dr. Sandy Baum and Dr. Patricia Steele of the Urban Institute, in 2015, only about 12% adults in the United States held advanced degrees [23]. In 1995, it was about 8%. I believe that this percentage will continue to increase, not because graduate programs are getting more enjoyable, but because the job market is becoming more competitive.

For doctors, pilots and other professions involved in safety and life, I agree that rigorous certification and standards must be achieved, but gatekeeping should be in residency or in-fly practice. Courses are for knowledge transfer, and for that reason, promoting internal self-motivation is far better than using strict external requirements. I believe that anyone can acquire any knowledge if he or she is motivated to do so. My cousin in Hong Kong got a rare disease. For a couple years, he went to several doctors, and his condition showed no signs of improving. He then decided to research it on his own. He spent a year reading all journal publications and conference proceedings related to the disease. He then suggested to the doctor which medication to try. The doctor took his advice and the disease was cured. This example case is not contingent on the recent internet and digital technology development. Centuries ago, the Chinese already had an idiom "a person with chronic diseases can become a good doctor" (久病成良醫). My cousin did not attend any courses related to medicine and clinical procedures while in school, but he became more knowledgeable on this particular disease than some experts in the field. This demonstrates the power of self-motivated education.

Therefore, education should focus on creating value for individuals, and content-centric systems are not the right approach. The ultimate objectives of education are: 1) to motivate students to learn, and 2) to teach them how to learn. Content design is merely a tool to achieve these objectives. As an instructor, I want to make the course content interesting. The usefulness of the content is not determined by the teacher. It is personal and depends on the needs of the students. In many of my courses, I usually conduct an exercise in which students participate at the beginning of the class to map the course topics. Then, I tailor the discussions to topics that are of interest to the students. I also spend more time choosing content delivery styles to make my classes enjoyable. All my courses have hands-on exercises and activities related to the content, targeting critical thinking and fun. If my students are looking forward to coming to my class, then the purpose is achieved. To quote Einstein again, "I never teach my pupils, I only provide the conditions in which they can learn."

> How to be an effective self-learner?

I hope more educators will agree with me, so that our education system will change. But until then, as a student, do not get frustrated because some courses are content-heavy and difficult. Take it on yourself to find out how to have fun and how to learn. Having fun will motivate you to learn. You can research and find fun facts and history about the topic to keep yourself interested. Find hands-on experiments and exercises that you can do to reflect the course content. Taking courses with friends who you have fun together will also make the course more enjoyable.

Self-learning Tips

- The focus of education: motivate to learn and learn how to learn
- Learn how to have fun in learning
    - Research and find fun facts about the topic
    - Conduct hands-on experiments and exercises
    - Do it with friends who you have fun together
    - Take fun elective courses
- Learn how to learn
    - Map the subject and the topics
    - Prepare questions
    - Reflect using metaphor, simile and analogy
    - Exercise all functions of your brain

Slide 75

You can also take a fun elective course and a difficult course together to improve the overall enjoyment, and it is better if the two courses are related. When I took the materials science course, I took a metal art course. I correlated the theory-focused content from the science course with hands-on metalsmith practices, making both courses enjoyable. While studying for the undergraduate engineering degree, I took many elective courses, such as filmmaking, ceramics, paint making and musical instrument, at least one every semester. These types of hands-on courses require little time outside the class hours, and it is relatively easy to get good grades. I did graduate with a lot more unit credits required for the degree, but these courses boosted my GPA and helped with the graduate school application.

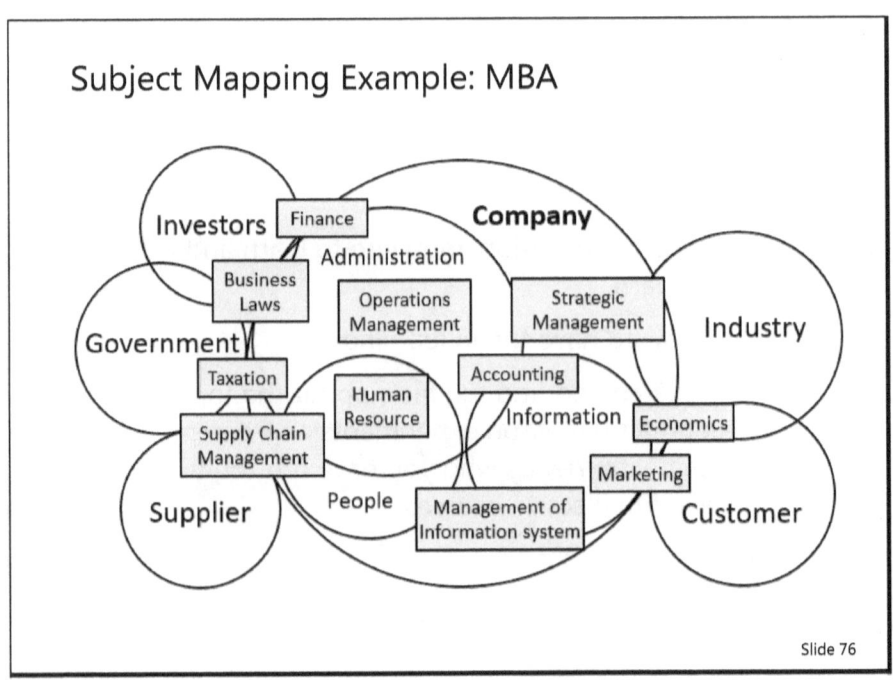

People tend to enjoy what they are good at. Therefore, it is important to learn how to learn and become a master self-learner. Here are some methods that I found useful. First, have a bigger picture of what you are going to learn. Before starting a course, map out the course in relation to other courses to form a holistic view of the subject. An example map for business administration is shown on Slide #76. Doing this mapping exercise helps you determine the order of the courses and understand where you are as the program progresses. More importantly, it forces you to think about the course and connect it to the real world. By the way, you are doing it in the context under your current knowledge, which promotes the triple-loop learning. You can continue to refine your map while learning the subject.

Next, review the syllabus of the course or the table of contents of the textbook, and then create a graphical map of the course using the covered topics. It serves a similar purpose as the subject map that we just discussed. Visual aids generally help us learn and retain knowledge. For me, this learning habit has carried on to teaching as a practice used in course design. Slide #77 shows the map of a project management course that I am teaching.

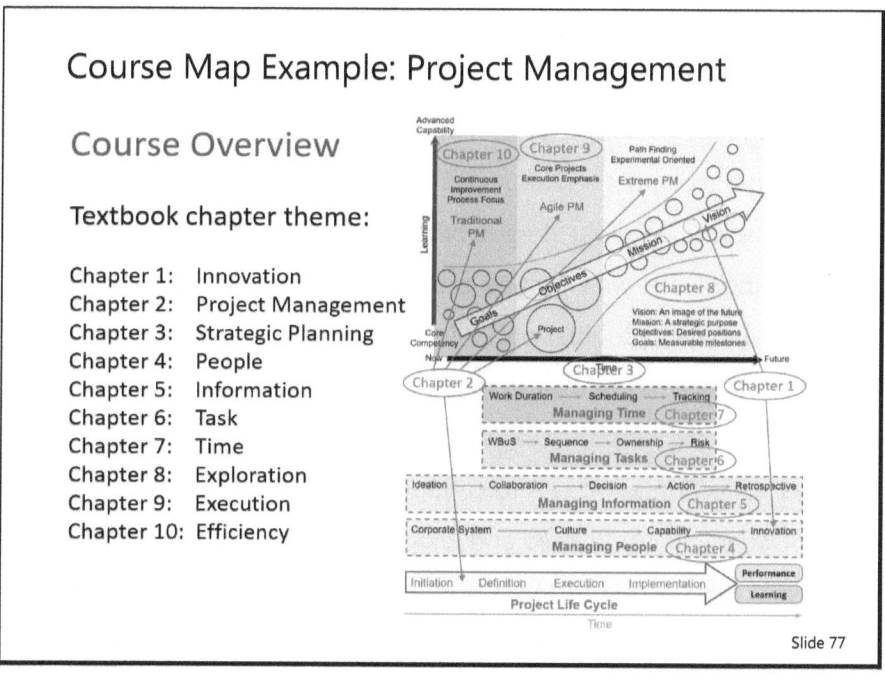

Before each class, review the course map and highlight the topics that will be covered, and write down the questions you have on the topic. I suggest that you have at least three questions. If you cannot find the answer from the lecture, ask the instructor. These questions should be the "why" and "how" questions, reflecting the triple-loop and double-loop learning. Avoid the single-loop "what" questions unless you really do not understand the concepts. You should search online to find answers to "what" questions, because these questions tend to be more straightforward. Again, the purpose of this exercise is to promote triple-loop learning and get to the practicality and the context of the topic.

Reflection is also critical for absorbing knowledge. This is why homework assignments are given in almost all courses. The purpose of homework is not only for grading, but also for reinforcing the learning. Even if homework assignment is not required for some topics and class sessions, you should still reflect on a newly learned concept. First, you can try to develop a metaphor, simile or analogy to explain the concept to an imaginary person who has no knowledge of the concept, such as explaining the computer operating system to a "grandma" (I am using one here and sorry about stereotyping). This exercise helps to connect the new knowledge with existing experience, thereby again promoting the triple-loop and double-loop learning. The best way to master a subject is actually to be able to teach it to someone.

Another reflection exercise is to critique the concepts. Find the opposite view of what you just learned and imagine how to debate the topic with the instructors and the textbook authors. It would be great if you have a close friend who can act as your opponent and actually debate with you. Of course, it may be difficult to draw the opposite view on certain topics, because they have been widely accepted. However, at some point in the past, people really believed the sun was circling around the earth until someone began to hold the opposite view. More recently, for over a century, people thought globalization was an inevitable trend, but now it has reversed. For topics that you do not find controversial, try to find inconsistencies, missing conditions and special cases where the concept is not readily applied. Many theories have limitations. Newton's law of gravity was regarded as an undisputed law of physics until Einstein expanded the concept to the larger universe. Consider how to apply the concept at the macro or micron level. In the earlier example of math addition used to explain triple-loop learning, we saw that many conditions 1 + 1 are not equal to 2. In addition to these conditions for teaching children, we also have "1+1=10" in the binary system, which is the basis of computer technology that has brought us into the information age and beyond. In reflecting a concept, think about special cases when certain elements are at zero or infinity. This exercise expands your mind to grasp new information.

Practicing and applying the concepts is also a great way to reflect on new knowledge. In certain topics, real-life experiments and hands-on practices are feasible, and conducting them personally can enhance your understanding of the concepts. Applying the learning to your own situation can also deepen your understanding and may bring real benefits to you.

When homework is required, getting good grades on the assignment depends on how reflective you are of the new learning. For essay type of assignments, in addition to demonstrate your understanding of the topic by reiterating the concept (single-loop learning), you need to apply it to real-life cases and analyze the findings (double-loop learning), and more importantly, offer your opinions and recommendations for improvement (triple-loop learning). In some social science and business courses, you can use your existing knowledge to do homework. In fact, you may not even need to attend classes and still offer a fair amount of opinions based on "common sense." Do not assume common sense is correct, and you need to refer to course materials to support your statements in the assignment. Your instructors will not feel good seeing that their teaching makes no difference on your intellect development.

You probably have heard of the left brain / right brain dichotomy, that is, the left brain is more active in logic and facts, and the right brain is more dominant in feelings and intuitions. This popular belief is challenged by others, who believe that a top brain / bottom brain distinction is more appropriate [24]. Others believe that the brain works in unity to produce thoughts and actions [25]. Although people have different views on which part of the brain performs what functions, we need to exercise these functions to learn at full capacity.

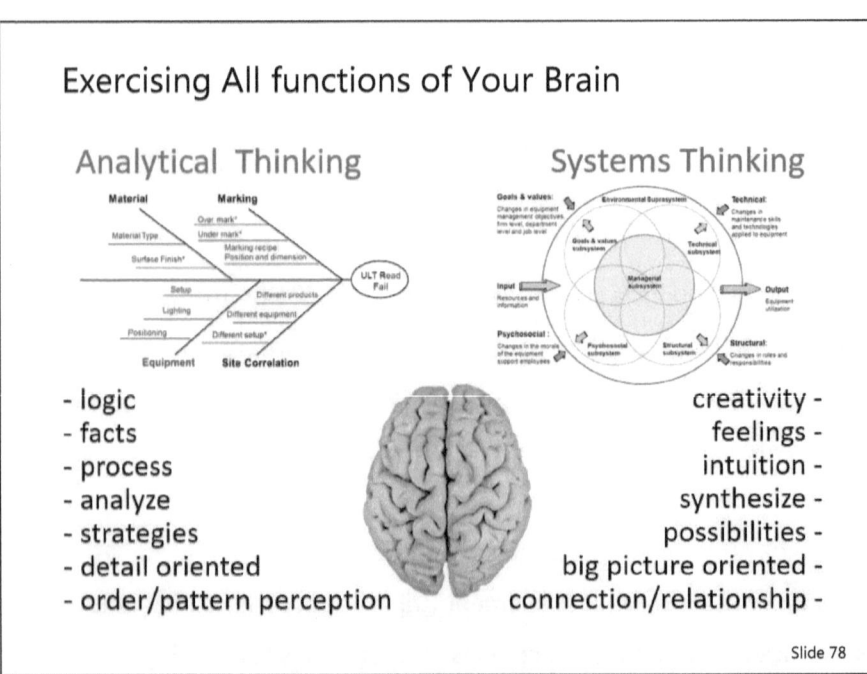

The content-centric curriculum design often focuses on exercising students' analytical thinking, which is mainly single-loop and double-loop learning. In order to pass such courses, students are usually required to answer the "what" questions. This means that single-loop learning is the primary focus of most students, because passing the courses are their first priority. Students who can apply the concepts to answer the "how" questions typically get good grades. Only a very small number of students can apply systems thinking to learn course contents.

Systems thinking is required for triple-loop learning. A well-known business theorist Peter Senge pointed out in his national bestselling book "*The Fifth Discipline*" that systems thinking is the most crucial discipline in developing learning capabilities [26]. This book is one of the must-read books I recommend. Although it is written for organizational learning, in addition to systems thinking, this book also covers personal mastery and mental models, which are useful knowledge for individuals.

Because systems thinking is rarely a part of the curriculum design, as a student, you need to bring system thinking into your learning process. All the exercises that I introduced earlier, mapping the subject and course topics, preparing "why" questions before classes, and reflecting newly learned concepts with a metaphor, simile or analogy, can promote systems thinking. Analytical thinking is still required to pass the courses, and systems thinking can bring fun to the otherwise rigid learning process, therefore, improving the quality and enjoyment of learning. Also, exercising all functions of your brain will increase your intellectual wellness.

In addition to applying system thinking to course contents, you can apply system thinking to bring creativity into the learning process. I developed an unconventional method to prepare for exams. Instead of studying in a quiet place such as a library, I watched TV while studying. I selected a movie or a film that I have watched once or twice but enjoy watching again. While studying the materials, the flow of the course content was corresponding to the plot of the movie. During the exam, I could recall the materials according to the storyline of the movie. This is an example of utilizing different functions of the brain to enhance the learning capability. Correlating the key concepts and formulas with the climaxes and interesting parts of the movie will achieve better results.

This method also enhances time management for exam preparation, i.e., the preparation of a chapter must be completed within the duration of the film. You can try this method, but I warn you that it takes practice and discipline. Depending on the subject of the course and the time required to prepare for the exam, you can also choose documentaries, comedy sitcoms, and even cartoons instead of movies. It is best to pick a category of films for a given type of subject, so that you can recall things more easily. You must also be disciplined to avoid focusing on watching the film instead of studying.

There are other brain function association tactics that can help you to memorize course materials. For example, I also tried eating something that I don't eat often while memorizing a difficult formula. You can try it and the food may be your favorite, least-liked, spicy or even bizarre like stinky tofu. When you exercise your brain, I believe you can develop creative learning methods that is suitable for you.

As I mentioned earlier, most courses are not designed with systems thinking. There are two main reasons. The first reason is that our education system is divided into disciplines and subjects with degree programs majoring in specific fields. The courses within a program are also divided by minors and specialties. This division of knowledge does not promote systems thinking characterized by holistic views and synthesis. For example, in most major universities, there is very little cooperation between their engineering school and business school, and joint courses taught by joint faculties hardly exist. In the real world, most businesses require both sets of skills to succeed.

The second reason is that we are bound by mental models, which is described as the second discipline in Peter Senge's book. Instructors are usually specialists in the topics that they teach. They often have advanced degrees and devote a significant amount of their lifetime on the specific topics. They need very strong beliefs to get this far. Such strong beliefs form mental models that unconsciously govern their behaviors and are difficult to change. Almost every instructor I had in the MBA program mentioned that his or her course was the most important subject in business. It was a way to convince the students to pay attention, and it was also a self-reinforcement of the worthiness of their tremendous dedication to these specific topics. Overemphasizing the value of one subject can limit the use of systems thinking in the classroom.

How to become an expert?

Becoming an expert is a career objective of many individuals. It takes time to become an expert. As I just described earlier, mental models are the result of this extensive process, and they are not necessarily conducive to further intellectual development. In the process of becoming an expert, you need to overcome the negative effects of the mental models set by existing experts. After being recognized as an expert, you also need to overcome the limitation set by your own mental models. One of my favorite books is "*The Structure of Scientific Revolutions*" by Thomas Kuhn. It was given to me at the beginning of my first doctorate program. Honestly, it changed my mindset and contributed significantly to the successful completion of multiple doctorate programs.

Dr. Kuhn states that the sciences progress through revolutionary paradigm shifts rather than the accumulation of puzzle-solving in an old paradigm [27]. To be considered valid, research studies are typically conducted with the approval of the experts in the paradigm. When a new concept or theory is proposed, the first reaction from the old paradigm is to scrutinize it, often with the intention of suppressing and discrediting it. Certainly, not all new concepts and theories are superior to the old ones, but they face a fair amount of skepticism. After all, if someone new to the field develops a better theory, this expert body is facing an identity crisis and will have difficulty maintaining the status quo. It is challenging for any paradigm to willingly accept its fault or incompleteness, and to surrender to a new challenger without a fight. The advancement of science is not only the result of experimentation, problem-solving and accumulation of knowledge, but also is greatly influenced by the mental models of experts.

As described by Dr. Kuhn, if you want to become an expert, you need to be accepted by the current expert community and be prepared to pass their scrutiny. This is not simply just a learning process only involving theoretical study, research and development. It requires interpersonal skills and persistence in order to overcome the limitations set by the mental models of the existing expert community.

Becoming an Expert

- Be prepared to overcome the negative effects of mental models set by existing expert community
    - Don't be frustrated with rejection
    - Be positive and persistence
    - Gain acceptance from the expert community
    - Develop professional relationships with experts
- Conduct rigorous research as if you are pursuing a doctorate program
    - Proper planning and discipline execution
    - Use analytical skills to fully comprehend the "box"
    - Apply systems thinking to connect adjacent fields and experiment outside-the-box solutions

Slide 79

I have experienced such limitations several times in my personal development journey. The topic I chose for my master thesis was rejected by two professors because it was considered too simple and not worth investigating. Although I strongly disagreed with their assessment, I decided not to spend energy to challenge them. I did my thesis according to their suggestions. They were very satisfied and provided excellent recommendations for my doctoral application. Later, the topic became the research focus for my doctoral dissertation and eventually turned into a book published by a major mainstream publisher.

These situations not only happen in universities. When I tried to publish a book on equipment management in 2011. The mainstream paradigm guiding equipment management was the discipline of maintenance management, which is governed by many associations. When a factory starts up, maintenance is customarily established as a functional department to maintain the equipment. Yet there is a fundamental flaw in the maintenance organizational structure: the departmental and individual objectives are not in sync with the factory objectives. Managers want to grow their departments to progress and survive in the corporate world, but doing so means a higher headcount and budget, which must be justified by a higher workload. Thus, growing the maintenance business means more downtime, either in the form of preventive maintenance or repairs, which reduces factory output due to equipment being offline. Conversely, if the manager achieves excellent equipment performance without any downtime, the maintenance department may be significantly reduced or no longer exist.

It is a dilemma that can only be addressed by moving away from the maintenance organizational structure. In addition, one of the main objectives of maintenance management - extending the life of equipment - is somewhat obsolete. It is a fact that in many high-tech companies, equipment replacement rarely occurs because of the end of the equipment's natural life. This new phenomenon is also seen in the general consumer market where most personal electronic devices, such as cell phones and computers, are replaced not because they are broken, but because a better version has arrived on the market.

I proposed that traditional maintenance management principles were no longer effective in the fast-changing business environment when I submitted my book proposal to the largest publisher in maintenance management. It caused quite a bit of disturbance and they rejected my proposal for "not wanting to alienate their reader base." Throughout the year-long review process, I built a professional relationship with the publisher's editor-in-chief. He supported me and wished that his organization "wasn't so conservative," so he recommended other publishers focused on factory productivity, and my book was finally published. Developing a new idea is exciting, but the process of getting acceptance is often accompanied with rejections. Don't be frustrated with rejection and use the interface opportunities to develop professional relationships instead.

In addition to being mentally prepared for the obstacles, proper planning and discipline execution are required to become an expert. I will demonstrate the process by sharing the approach I used to complete multiple doctoral programs. Getting a doctorate degree is characteristically challenging with approximately 50 percent of doctoral students withdrawing from the programs without getting the degree [28]. This is not just about coming up with new ideas, but also the process of developing and proving the ideas. Doctoral students are under tremendous pressure, and from my experience in obtaining multiple doctorate degrees, people who are disciplined in the process have a greater chance of success. In 2015, I was asked by UC Berkeley to design a course to help Ph.D. students increase their chances of getting the degree. The following content covers the key recommendations of this course.

Doctoral programs are time-bound with many milestones that must be met under relatively strict timelines. Most universities have a 7-year limit to finish the program, but you should plan to complete it in 4 to 5 years. The majority of graduate students find doctoral programs quite intense with many activities to be done in a short period of time. Completing a doctoral program demands early planning on key activities. The illustration shown on Slide #80 is the path I recommend to doctoral students, which is also a process of accumulating knowledge over time.

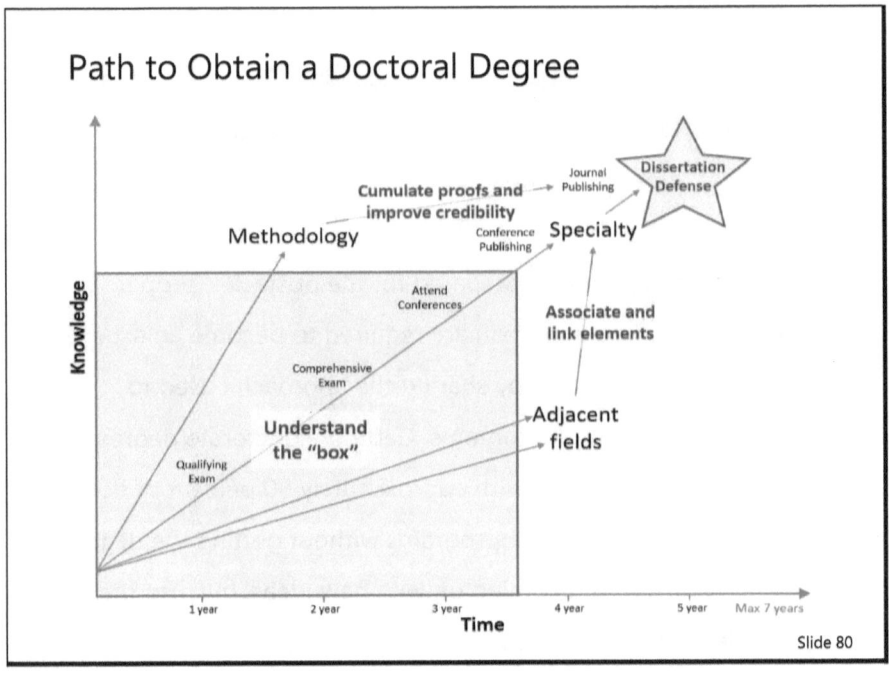

Slide 80

Planning the entire program provides you with a high-level roadmap. I also recommend that students make an annual plan every year. The illustration on Slide #81 shows the recommended activities for the first year. In addition to the coursework needed to reach the first major milestone, the qualifying exam, many other research activities are necessary to ensure the success of the entire program. Many doctoral students make the mistake of going through the first couple of years of doctoral programs as bachelor's and master's programs by only focusing on coursework. They would typically face difficulty in meeting the research and publication timelines in the later part of the program. Coursework and research are interrelated, and the knowledge gained in the courses supports the research.

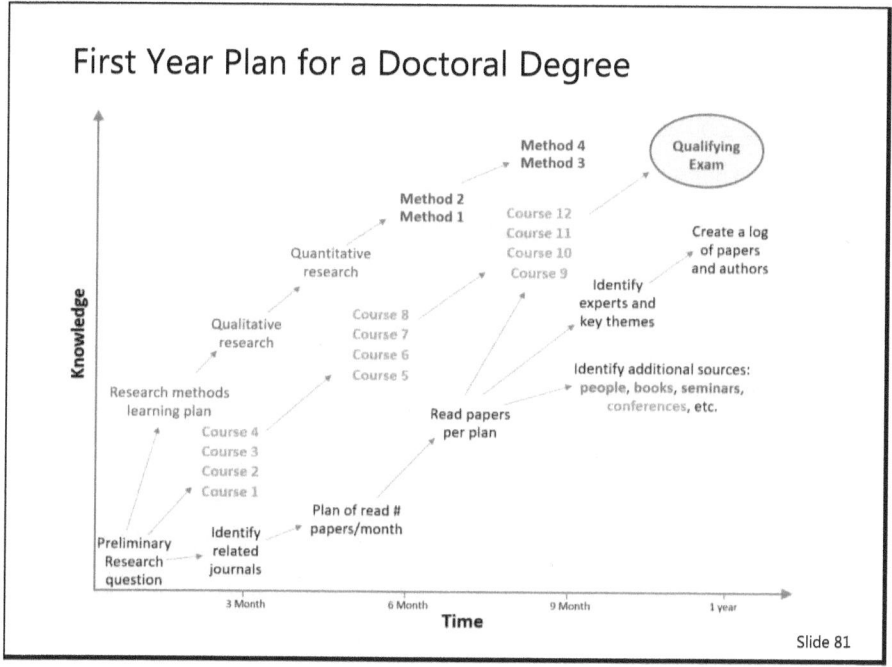

The first-year activities are part of the process of understanding the "box" shown in Slide #80. The "box" refers to the existing knowledge in the field. Not only does the subject specialty need to be learned, the methodology used to prove the current theory must be studied as well. In fact, the learning curve of the methodology needs to happen at a faster pace. Based on the triple-loop learning discussed earlier, effective learning occurs when the underlying assumptions and the context of the theory are fully understood. Knowing how others derived the theory helps you to comprehend the theory as well as develop strategies to prove your own theories.

In addition, understanding theories in the adjacent fields will broaden their perspectives; many innovative solutions are a fusion of knowledge from multiple fields. Systems thinking is applied to connect and synthesize the findings from various fields. When your research project is initiated, the first phase is to learn the existing solution "box," which includes all the existing practices, the methods used to develop these solutions, and practices in similar fields. For example, if you are developing a better cleaning method for semiconductor manufacturing, you should research all the existing cleaning methods, how each cleaning method is developed and processed, and the cleaning methods from other industries that also require cleaning, such as cleaning methods used in surgery, dentistry and maybe even archaeology.

The process of understanding the 'box" consists of rigorous research and requires disciplined detection and organization of information. It is a process of building a database of existing solutions. Analytical skills are being used here to analyze the facts, orders and patterns. Until the "box" is fully comprehended, no one can be certain that your new idea is truly outside-the-box. Sometimes, you may find a proposed solution has already been done by others, or an existing method actually produces better results than the proposed solution, all of which are normal. You should then seek the next solution or drop this particular method as a support in your research. Only solutions that have potential to go outside of the "box" will continue to the next phase for experiments and further study.

When you believe that you have a full understanding of the "box" and are ready to present the findings, you can request a review session with your doctoral committee. If you have some decision power on forming the committee, pick the people you trust and work well with you. In many universities, in addition to your professors, one or two experts from the industry are allowed to be on your doctoral committee. When this is the case, you should invite industry experts to join your doctoral committee. A qualified and reputable committee is crucial because it can ensure that your work is indeed outside-the-box. Having experts from the industry can cover the latest developments as well as areas that are not accessible to academia. It can also increase your connection with the workplace for future benefits in career advancement. It would be better if the industry expert is someone already in your professional network. Generally, choosing your own committee members can increase your influence on the committee.

Once your research proposal passes the gatekeepers and exits the "box," you should work with the doctoral committee to set the ideal end target date of finishing your research as well as the timeline for achieving that target. You need to proactively setup regular review sessions with your doctoral committee to review experiment results and track progress to the milestones. Another function of the doctoral committee is to provide guidance and resources for you. Seek advice and ask for help in connecting you to laboratories and facilities required for your research. Trust your doctoral committee and avoid challenging them. If you have a strong disagreement with them, present your point with reliable data and solid support. You can reserve your disagreement for future research after completing the degree, at such time when you are accepted to be part of the expert community.

Building an expert reputation at work follows the similar process. You need to understand the "box" of your responsible area at work, which means mastering all tools, methods and practices used in the area. Learn the processes and tools of the adjacent areas, including the suppliers and receivers of your area. Solve issues from their perspective to improve your area and integrate the entire value chain. You must also develop outside-the-box innovations to be considered an expert. All these actions can help you gain the technical skills of an expert, but this is not enough. More importantly, you also need to develop the right attitude of an expert. Earn credibility among your peers before challenging them openly. Avoid building a paradigm with mental models that limit yourself and others. Listen to all viewpoints, don't be over skeptical of new ideas, and don't overreact to others' failures. Be approachable and establish a good reputation as the go-to person not only for technical problems but also for advice and encouragement. Share your knowledge with others and learn training, coaching and mentoring skills to effectively develop your team.

The Right Attitude of an Expert

- Avoid building a paradigm with mental models that limit yourself and others
- Listen to all viewpoints
    - Don't be over skeptical of new ideas
    - Don't overreact to others' failures
- Be approachable and establish a good reputation as the go-to person
    - Solving technical problems
    - Providing advice and encouragement
- Share your knowledge and learn training, coaching and mentoring skills

Slide 82

> How about improving resume, cover letter and interview?

Many people only start looking for a career advisor when they are looking for a job. For most career advisors, reviewing resumes and helping prepare for interviews are the most frequent requests form people. For those who seek such help in my book, I am sorry that you have to read this far to get to this point. I am doing this for a couple reasons. First, I think these are the activities that you can learn well, and they are great exercises after you learn how to be a self-learner. Second, increasing internal value should come before improving external packaging. As a career advisor, I would rather take the time to help you become a stronger candidate, rather than make you more presentable through sugar-coating.

Now that we have covered the learning process, I will provide you with general guidance to improve your resume and cover letter writing and interview skills. Put yourself in the position of hiring manager, what kind of candidates would you hire? We covered this on Page 134 when managing down was discussed. Managers are looking for subordinates with ability, willingness and confidence. Willingness and confidence are more important than ability, because if a person is willing to learn and has confidence to try, he or she will eventually gain a certain level of ability. How do you demonstrate your willingness and confidence to the hiring manager? Obviously, this is not from your resume. A resume just shows your ability.

Therefore, before you have a chance for the interview, the only thing that reveals your willingness and confidence is the cover letter. Your cover letter should not be just a summary of the abilities shown on your resume. It needs to show your motivation for doing this job and your confidence in achieving good results. How do you write your cover letter? You can follow the SMART reporting guide on Page 143-145. Straightforward means be direct and concise. Don't send the letter as an attachment. Type your letter directly in the email window. Memorable means making your letter standout and making an impression. Think about how to use unconventional formats and writing styles to catch the reader's attention. Action-oriented means showing what you can do and what you will do when you are given the opportunity, which demonstrates willingness and confidence. Relevance means tailoring your letter for different recipients, customizing for HR personnel, the direct supervisor, and next-level managers. Timely means sending the letter as soon as you know the position is available.

SMART reporting also applies to your resume writing but may take difference forms. Here is where you practice triple-loop learning as the context of a resume is different from a cover letter. Straightforward in your resume means being concise, that is, use bullet points instead of complete sentences and avoid pretty but meaningless adjectives. You do need to send the resume as an attachment as is the custom. The format and layout of your resume greatly enhance the reader's impression of you. Convert it to a pdf file so that the format will appear as intended. Start each bullet with a verb to show the action, using present tense for current activities and past tense for previous positions. Do not write them as a duty list. Use the "so what" test to add impact after the action. You also need to tailor your resume to the position by placing the most relevant information near the top. Study the job description and add keywords to match the job description as much as possible. For both cover letter and resume, avoid using a standard template and just change the company name and the position. Any experienced manager can tell that you did not put in much effort, which indicates very little willingness. If you do not treat the position as special, why should they give you the opportunity?

As far as interview preparation is concerned, most of the materials covered in this book will help you. Use the TOP model to show your passion and talent to convince the interviewers that the position is your dream job. Ask the interviewers the opportunities offered by the company to confirm that the position is indeed your dream job. An interview is mutual. Have your career plan drafted because most interviewers will ask you about your future career perspectives. On Page 86 in the task management session, we have discussed about identifying ways to exceed the expectations of the interviewers. The micromessage concept described on Page 135-137 can help you understand non-verbal cues from interviewers, as well as watch out for the unintended micromessages you send by dressing, greeting and reacting to inquiries. Of course, use SMART reporting as well. You can also use the influence tactics described on Page 124-128 to influence the interviewers. Anyway, practice the learning tactics in this session to improve your interview skills. Most career advisors will advise you to be yourself in the interview, so improving yourself is the best answer.

> What if I am done being a student?

Learning and education is a lifelong journey. Some people have a good start by getting into good universities such as Ivy League schools or

Stanford, while others may start with community colleges. Don't compare yourself to others. This journey is like a marathon. It doesn't matter whether you are ahead of everyone or behind others at the beginning. In fact, it doesn't matter at any time before reaching the finish line, and the finish line is defined by you. As long as you continue to run, you will go further than those who have stopped. Even after you become an expert, you will be surpassed if you stop learning.

You need to enjoy learning when you are doing it over a lifetime, and you should also pace yourself for a long run. For me, I find enjoyment in the way that suits me. When I was in high school and undergraduate college, according to most people's standards, especially my Chinese relatives and friends, I was not a good student because I lacked focus and played too much. It took me about six years to get a bachelor's degree as I changed my major several times, from Electrical Engineering to Mechanical Engineering then to Industrial Engineering. I took many non-required courses such as filmmaking, metal art, ceramics, photography, music history, Chinese painting, plus many sports course such as golf, soccer, tennis, badminton, swimming, etc. These allowed me to enjoy school and laid the foundation for the continuation of graduate school, and eventually obtaining doctorate degrees in business and engineering in the later years.

Learning does not end when I was done with school as a student. The best way to master a subject is actually to teach it. As an instructor, I have learned so much by designing and teaching different courses, not just the content, but also the teaching methods as well as the interests and needs of the students in order to effectively create value for them. I started to teach computer and software courses at San Jose State

University about twenty years ago, then at Santa Clara University, University of San Francisco, University of Hong Kong and finally Stanford University. The courses covered undergraduate and graduate from engineering school to business school. Each change represented an improvement and development of my skills. Again, my focus is to design the courses that are enjoyable for the students and for me too. To me, being educated and educating others are occurring simultaneously, and when I am teaching a subject, the highest level of learning occurs.

Similarly, I learned a great deal about career development after I became a career advisor. By sharing my experience and writing this book, my thoughts are better organized and will make me to be a better advisor. I hope the experience and knowledge I shared will be helpful to you.

Session 6 Summary: Learning and Education

- Learning reduces fear and comfort, thereby promoting growth
- Continuing education through degree or certificate programs, open university and online courses, corporate training and personal coaches
- Learn how to learn using triple-loop learning, applying systems thinking in addition to analytical thinking
- Become an expert, not only focus on acquiring technical skills, but also having the right attitude
- Learning continues to extend from being educated to educating others

Slide 83

THIS IS NOT

THE END

Share your thoughts with me via email
Kerngpeng@gmail.com

Session 6 Exercise #1 – Build a course study guide

Step 1. Map the subject (Map the course in relations to other courses)

Subject: _____ (See example on Slide #76)

Step 2. Identify the key topics of the course

List the key topics of the course: (find the information on syllabus or use the textbook chapter titles)

Topics	Lecture Date	Assessment*

* Your current knowledge or difficulty of the topic

Step 3. Map the course (Connect the topics)

Course: _____ (See example on Slide #77)

Step 4. Prepare questions before each class and take notes in class

Class meeting: _____
Covered Topics: _____
(Prefer "why" questions over "how" and "what" questions)

Q#1 _____
    Note: _____
    _____

Q#2 _____
    Note: _____
    _____

Q#3 _____
    Note: _____
    _____

Step 5. Reflect on new learning, severing as an assignment guide to be competed in class or as soon as possible after class

Title of the concept: _____

Summary of the concept
Reiterate the concept in your own words

Metaphor/Simile/Analogy

Critiques
Opposite views:

Inconsistencies:

Limitations:

Special cases:

Applications and Practices
How this concept can be applied in real-life and in your situation?

Opinions and Recommendations

Step 6. Develop an exam study plan

List the topics of the course: (Information on the first row of each topic is from Step 2 of the exercise)

Topics	Lecture Date	Assessment
Key concepts:	Study time:	Method:
Key concepts:	Study time:	Method:
Key concepts:	Study time:	Method:
Key concepts:	Study time:	Method:
Key concepts:	Study time:	Method:
Key concepts:	Study time:	Method:
Key concepts:	Study time:	Method:
Key concepts:	Study time:	Method:
Key concepts:	Study time:	Method:
Key concepts:	Study time:	Method:

Session 6 Exercise #2 - Planning a research

Step 1. Determine the research questions and hypotheses

Research Title: _____

Research Question	Hypothesis

Step 2. Understand current approaches and methods

Literature Review		
Author(s): Publisher: Date:	Hypothesis: Conclusions:	Research method: Conditions:
Author(s): Publisher: Date:	Hypothesis: Conclusions:	Research method: Conditions:
Author(s): Publisher: Date:	Hypothesis: Conclusions:	Research method: Conditions:

* Add new rows for addition literature. Need to research and cover all literature with research question similar to yours

Step 3. Determine research methods (Multiple methods preferred)

Methods*	Desired Data	Time Needed

* Key methods: experiment, correlation, survey, interview, case study, focus group, direct observation and records

Step 4. Identify adjacent areas for comparison

Areas	Similarities	Differences

Step 5. Use the following checklist for data analysis and association

Data Analysis
- ☐ Data organization
- ☐ Data categorization
- ☐ Data interpretation
- ☐ Patterns & uniqueness
- ☐ Inconsistency & anomalies

Data Association
- ☐ Correlation to existing theories
- ☐ Correlation to previous studies
- ☐ Correlation to your hypotheses
- ☐ Relation to adjacent areas
- ☐ Surprises & special cases

Conclusion
- ☐ Clear answers to research questions
- ☐ Lesson learned
- ☐ Values created
- ☐ Follow-on studies
- ☐ Recommendation on utilizing your theory
- ☐ Recommendation for execute steps
- ☐ Trends & predictions
- ☐ Follow-on studies

Index by Question

Session 1, question 1 — Page 2
What is career? What is career development? Why take ownership of career development?

Session 1, question 2 — Page 4
What are the key components of a successful career? What is the TOP model in career development?

Session 1, question 3 — Page 5
What are the characteristics of the talent circle? How should an individual manage his or her talent circle?

Session 1, question 4 — Page 7
What are the natural strengths? How do you assess your strengths?

Session 1, question 5 — Page 8
What are the characteristics of the opportunity circle? How should an individual recognize the opportunity circle?

Session 1, question 6 — Page 11
What are the specific actions that an individual could take to increase his or her awareness?

Session 1, question 7 — Page 12
What are the characteristics of the passion circle? How should we define the passion circle?

Session 1, question 8 — Page 14
How to establish the passion circle?

Session 1, question 9 — Page 17
How to apply the TOP model in career development?

Session 2, question 1 — Page 22
What is a career vision? Why is a career vision important?

Session 2, question 2 — Page 23
How does an individual identify and develop a career vision?

Session 2, question 3 — Page 25
What does a good career plan look like?

Session 2, question 4 — Page 27
What are the specific considerations in developing the long-term activities in a career plan?

Session 2, question 5 — Page 31
What are the specific considerations in developing the mid-term activities in a career plan?

Session 2, question 6 — Page 34
What are the specific considerations in developing the short-term activities in a career plan?

Session 2, question 7 — Page 36
How to consolidate activities and present them as one career plan?

Session 3, question 1 — Page 46
Why is time management so important?

Session 3, question 2 — Page 47
What are the common drawbacks in mainstream time management methods?

Session 3, question 3 — Page 49
What are the bad behaviors to avoid in time management?

Session 3, question 4 — Page 55
Do you know how you spend time and why is it important for you to know?

Session 3, question 5 — Page 58
How to make time?

Session 3, question 6 — Page 62
What are the key points in practicing the unconventional time management method proposed in this book?

Session 4, question 1 — Page 72
What is task management?

Session 4, question 2 — Page 73
What is the priority matrix method, and should you use it?

Session 4, question 3 — Page 75
What is the time-based prioritization method, and when should it be used?

Session 4, question 4 — Page 80
What are the pros and cons of the time-based prioritization method?

Session 4, question 5 — Page 83
How to design a task plan to achieve exceptional results?

Session 4, question 6 — Page 87
How to initiate tasks and determine their impact?

Session 4, question 7 — Page 91
What is risk management?

Session 4, question 8 — Page 94
When to contain risks and when to take risks? And how?

Session 4, question 9 — Page 98
What is the process flow for task management?

Session 5, question 1 — Page 108
What are the main components of a good work environment?

Session 5, question 2 — Page 109
How to determine if a company suits your personality and work style?

Session 5, question 3 — Page 111
What are the key elements in managing professional relations?

Session 5, question 4 — Page 112
How to prioritize your networking effort?

Session 5, question 5 — Page 114
How to seek networking opportunities inside your company?

Session 5, question 6 — Page 117
How to find external networking opportunities?

Session 5, question 7 — Page 120
How to maintain professional relationships?

Session 5, question 8 — Page 124
What are the influence tactics?

Session 5, question 9 — Page 128
How to manage up, across and down working relationships?

Session 5, question 10 — Page 135
How to improve your communication at the workplace?

Session 5, question 11 — Page 135
How to communicate effectively through non-verbal cues?

Session 5, question 12 — Page 137
How to effectively manage meetings?

Session 5, question 13 — Page 143
How to write a good report?

Session 5, question 14 — Page 145
How to prepare for and deal with difficult situations?

Session 5, question 15 — Page 146
How to solve a problem effectively?

Session 5, question 16 — Page 150
How to make the right decision?

Session 6, question 1 — Page 162
Why is continuous learning important?

Session 6, question 2 — Page 164
What are the means of continuing education?

Session 6, question 3 — Page 169
What are the different levels of learning?

Session 6, question 4 — Page 171
What exactly is education?

Session 6, question 5 — Page 174
How to be an effective self-learner?

Session 6, question 6 — Page 183
How to become an expert?

Session 6, question 7 — Page 193
How about improving resume, cover letter and interview?

Session 6, question 8 — Page 195
What if I am done being a student?

Bibliography

1. Lia Taylor (2018). *Life on TOP*. The Decisive Data Blog. URL: https://www.decisivedata.net/blog/life-top

2. Marcus Buckingham & Donald O. Clifton (2001). *Now, Discover Your Strengths*. The Free Press

3. David Epstein (2014). *Are the Athletes Really Getting Faster, Better, Stronger*. TED. URL: https://www.ted.com/talks/david_epstein_are_athletes_really_getting_faster_better_stronger#t-53545

4. Gartner (2017). *Gartner Hype Cycle*. Research Methodologies, Gartner. URL: https://www.gartner.com/technology/research/methodologies/hype-cycle.jsp

5. Kaye Lean Ramos (2017). *9 Late Bloomer Success Stories Who Prove It's Never Too Late to Achieve Your Dreams: Success Despite Age*. Mission.org. URL: https://medium.com/the-mission/9-late-bloomer-success-stories-who-prove-its-never-too-late-to-achieve-your-dreams-b036688da6f

6. George T. Doran (1981). *There's a S.M.A.R.T. way to write managements's goals and objectives*. Management Review, AMA Forum

7. Cyril Northcote Parkinson (1955). *Parkinson's Law*. The Economist

8. Don Reinertsen (2009). *Principles of Product Development Flow: Second Generation Lean Product Development*. Celeritas Publishing.

9. Scaled Agile (2020). *Weighted Shortest Job First*. URL: http://www.scaledagileframework.com/wsjf/

10. Aberdeen Group (2006). *Onboarding Benchmarking Report*.

11. Situation Management Systems, Inc. (1987). *Positive Power and Influence Program*. 3rd Edition Participant Workbook.

12. The Myers & Briggs Foundation (2018). *MBTI Basics.* URL: https://www.myersbriggs.org/my-mbti-personality-type/mbti-basics/

13. Your Life's Path (2018). *DiSC Classic 2.0.* URL: https://www.thediscpersonalitytest.com/

14. Paul Hersey, Kenneth H. Blanchard & Dewey E. Johnson (1996). *Management of Organizational Behavior.* 7rd Edition. Prentice Hall.

15. Stephen Young (2016). *Micromessaging: Why Great Leadership is Beyond Words.* McGraw-Hill Education

16. Cindy Perman (2012). *Hate Meetings? Why Most Are Complete Failures.* CNBC. URL: https://www.cnbc.com/id/48898453

17. Andrea Lehr (2015, updated 2017). *Why We Hate Meetings So Much [Infographic].* Hubspot. URL: https://blog.hubspot.com/sales/why-we-hate-meetings-so-much

18. John Walston (2015). *Finally! The Truth About Why We Hate Meetings [Infographic].* ResourcefulManager. URL: https://www.resourcefulmanager.com/why-do-we-hate-meetings/

19. Kern Peng (2019). *Project management for Continuous Innovation.* Pike Publications

20. Andrew S. Grove (2015). *High Output Management.* Vintage

21. George T. Doran (1981). *There's a S.M.A.R.T. way to write managements's goals and objectives.* Management Review, AMA Forum

22. Chris Argyris & Donald A. Schön (1996). *Organizational Learning II: Theory, Method and Practice. Reading.* Addison-Wesley

23. Sandy Baum & Patricia Steele (2017). *Who Goes to Graduate School and Who Succeeds?* The Urban Institute

24. Stephen Kosslyn & G. Wayne Miller (2013). *Top Brain, Bottom Brain: Surprising Insights into How You Think.* Simon & Schuster

25. Joseph B. Hellige (2001). *Hemispheric Asymmetry: What's Right and What's Left.* Harvard University Press

26. Peter M. Senge (2006). *The Fifth Discipline: The art and practice of the learning organization.* 2nd Edition. Image Books

27. Thomas S. Kuhn (1996). *The Structure of Scientific Revolutions.* 3rd Edition. University of Chicago Press

28. Leonard Cassuto (2013). *Ph.D. Attrition: How Much Is Too Much?* The Chronicle of Higher Education. URL: https://www.chronicle.com/article/PhD-Attrition-How-Much-Is/140045

www.ingramcontent.com/pod-product-compliance
Lightning Source LLC
Chambersburg PA
CBHW021100080526
44587CB00010B/316